Core Pillars

A path to creating balance and perspective

Robert Maxwell

Table of Contents

Proceeds will go to the Irish Heart Foundation

Prologue

My book *Core Pillars* is a non-fiction self-help narrative written to assist people struggling with difficulties and looking to rediscover themselves. The work is a condensed collection of my personal journaling and reflections over a number of years. The target audience is for people interested in improving their quality of life, particularly those of working age who are curious about maximising their potential both professionally and personally. Those who are interested in psychology and behavioural economics can also enjoy this book.

The book is divided into eight equal parts or chapters namely Self, Mind, Habits, Failure, Health, Wellbeing, Purpose, and Money. Each part represents an important component of the overall *Core Pillars*, and I explore the idea that one cannot feel fully fulfilled without all parts working in harmony. I give lots of scientifically backed examples and useful exercises throughout the book to help the reader reflect on their own particular situation. Equally, many of the chapters draw on behavioural economics and positive psychology studies in order to support a claim, such as holding a warm drink in hand can influence how you feel about a person! I try to focus on key topics which most people can relate to in their own daily life, and often share my own personal experiences and setbacks as part of the reader's journey.

I believe this book can play a role in boosting morale and self-reflection during this time of widespread economic pain and emotional suffering. Topics such as the importance of quality relationships, understanding how our mind can influence our thoughts, the limitations of money in boosting our happiness above a certain threshold, and the significance of having a purpose day to day, are all explored in depth among many other subjects relevant to all of us, yet often overlooked in today's hyper materialistic and uber competitive society.

The goal is to share a collection of counsel I received so far in my life which in hindsight, I wish I had known earlier. Through conversations with people of all stages in life, I believe we can learn a lot about common challenges which underpin our collective spirit. It is this knowledge sharing between generations that is so often overlooked in society despite its value. From personal finance and healthcare, to relationships, suffering, and even technology, there is so much we can bring to the table by better understanding ourselves and engaging with others!

Now is a good time to start given the ongoing uncertainty around the Covid-19 pandemic. Thus far many people find themselves out of work and out of pocket, putting strain on mental wellbeing and savings, which will likely mean working harder and for longer before retirement. Even the front-line healthcare workers are finding the going tough, with a recent YouGov poll in the UK showing over 50% suffered a deterioration in mental health since the pandemic struck. Worse still, others are suffering in silence and isolation, either struggling to get their daily supplies or battling the virus symptoms, or both. Mental resilience will be key to overcoming these increasing strains, and if this book can resonate with one person in hardship or hoping to turn a corner, it will have been worthwhile to put pen to paper.

Going forward, many experts believe that these viruses are more likely to occur given the world today is increasingly globalised and inter-connected. As a result, we need to have a toolkit of readily available behaviours and habits we can quickly adapt in order to improve our wellbeing and resilience to such stressful situations. In my view, a crucial part of developing resilience is building a strong, reliable network to offer support and words of encouragement when needed, because let's face it, we all do from time to time!

This book will work to help identify your core values and map out the life you want to enjoy. Some of the key reflection points include dreaming big, positive psychology, contemplating how you want to live and spend your time, identifying influences you want to surround yourself with, and activities to pursue outside of your overarching purpose. Happiness is said to be a combination of purpose and pleasure so it is really important to find the right balance between the two, and not a lopsided scale with all the weight hanging on one side. Visualise your perfect day, optimal surroundings, and ideal life - this is the first step toward realising it!

PART I

SELF

DON'T JUDGE A BOOK BY ITS COVER

You've tried your best but it's not enough. The world can be so competitive and isolating it begs the question of why we are here and how we should model our best self. One can do a doctorate in philosophy and still not have the answer to such questions. In fact, there are many leaders in society today who appear to have it all on first glance, but when we learn more about them, the fact is many are struggling with the same issues we are, whether it be happiness, health, purpose, pleasure, money, family, or relationships. As a result, it can difficult to know who to look up to. Some have failed in business or politics; others have lost face or moved on to their third marriage in quick succession. Now I am certainly not suggesting the reason for the marriage break-up was their fault necessarily, however when it happens for the third and fourth time, it may be a hint to start some self-reflection in my view. In fact, the research shows after one marriage break-up the probability goes up and not down the next marriage will also end in break-up and so forth!

Coming back to the point, life is about having fun and making the most of the time you have in front of you. Unfortunately, or fortunately, depending on your outlook, life doesn't go on forever and we have a fixed amount of time to make an impact and play a role for the betterment of the next generation. How one goes about this is a personal choice. Some will do their best to make a positive impact on society, while others will do their own thing, perhaps benefiting from a large inheritance. These are personal decisions and the great thing is there is no right or wrong answer here. From a moral perspective however, I do believe we each have an obligation to make a positive contribution if we are in a position to do so. Whether this be through community service, volunteering, or of course professional life is up to us. One can argue working as a doctor is slightly more impactful than working as a lawyer for example. However, the point is we can turn any role into a benefit for society through the way we go about it and the contributions we make as a result of our position. While a doctor is out on the front-line saving lives on a daily basis, a lawyer can claim to defend innocent people and help restore justice and ethics in society. Regardless of the role, we can all play a part to make the world a better place for others and the next generation. Not only this, but having a purpose in life also makes you happier as we will touch on later in this book. Time and time again, we see examples of people in society who decide to retire early and don't know what to do with themselves. After a short time, many of them go back to work as there is only so much time one can spend on the golf course or working on DIY projects!

FORM YOUR OWN VIEW

While this can be a sensitive subject, I believe it is important we all have a view on our life philosophy. In my opinion, the vast majority of us go by in life without placing a second thought to our meaning or role in the bigger picture. Rather, we have too many distractions, and as we rush through our day we fail to stop, smell the roses, and take a deep breath.

I recently came across an interesting statistic which suggested that the more intelligent you are, the more likely you are to be an atheist. I was perplexed initially but having reflected on the statement it began to make sense. It is the more intelligent and curious persons who question the status quo to better understand their life philosophy and form their own opinion on higher powers. The vast majority of us including myself typically inherit our religious beliefs from our parents who in turn receive their life philosophy from preceding ancestors. It is our culture and location on the map that overwhelmingly determines our beliefs, political stance and other factors rather than our independent research and curiosity to form our own view. As I see it, this is something that needs to change and is adapting gradually led by the younger generations. For example, a recent poll in the US showed Harvard University had among the highest number of students in the country who classified themselves as atheists. This would have been unimaginable 30 or 40 years ago however in today's society it is seen as a mark of intellectual curiosity rather than ignorance. Interestingly many of the millennial generation would consider themselves to be very spiritual but not religious. In other words, they see themselves living in relationship with or alongside a God or Higher Power, but not necessarily believing in one. Growing up in my own community, I remember any self-proclaimed atheist would be classified as lost or confused. However, today this is no longer the case which is a positive step to encourage independent thinking, and the same should be practiced across all areas of life including sexual preferences, profession, and hobbies among others.

DISCOVER YOUR PACE

The difficult part of growing up is that while older people advise it should be the most enjoyable time of your life with little responsibility, at the same time you are trying hard to figure out who you are and what you want in life without much support. As you evolve through your teenage years, you become smarter about how to manage expectations, bounce back from rejections, and manage your health and wellbeing. You gain the necessary perspective to understand nothing comes easy in life and relationships come and go. You begin to learn to adapt to life's constantly changing circumstances and develop a sense of perspective that not everything will work out as planned. It is also a time to build your true friends and quality relationships. Many of these people will come into your life during your teenage years and so it is crucial you are in a positive state of mind to choose the right influences. The old saying, 'you are the average of the 5 people you spend most time with' strikes a chord with me. For most big moments, we only get one shot to make a decision or an impression, so it is critical we are clear headed and have the right blend of external counsel to confide in. Everybody wants validation in terms of our job, industry practice, friends, and relationships. And in the absence of being able to validate ourselves we turn to others for validation. This is why surrounding yourself with inspiring friends and those who bring the best out of you become so important. As the saying goes, 'show me your friends and I'll tell you who you are!'

I often reflect on an anecdote I use to determine whether I am in control of my situation in times of stress. I think about a small canoe padding through the choppy river full of treacherous twists and turns. I ask myself, am I controlling the speed and direction, or am I being taken for a ride? Am I navigating the various obstacles such as rocks and trees or am I out of my depth with little control of the steering and likely to lose control at any moment? If the latter is true then I need to promptly take action before the situation gets worse. The point is life is there for the taking through our control and precision, without which we can quickly lose course. Small things like the day of the week too often determine our mood and focus for no apparent reason other than psychological. We feel grumpy on a Monday and ready to have a good time on Thursday and Friday; we need to take control of ourselves to feel energised every day!

PURPOSEFUL PRACTICE

Growing up I was a pretty average kid. My mum was a keen tennis player and she instilled an interest in both myself and my brother from an early age. My earliest memories were that I was not very good at the sport. I spent a lot of time in the local tennis club playing with friends however I was not particularly talented and far from the best player in my age category. In fact, I remember very well the person who was better than me at under 8s and 10s age level. While he enjoyed the sport and continued to play every summer, I quickly surpassed the others because I became obsessed with hitting balls day and night. My parents were very supportive to help my interest blossom and dropped me to the tennis club after school every other day. So much so that the tennis club became my 'babysitter' which was very convenient for my parents as there was no babysitting charges which as we all know can really add up! At the same time, I began taking lessons and remember attending regular group classes through the dark winter months.

Roll the clock forward three years and I was winning provisional and national tennis singles and doubles events. Why was this the case? It certainly wasn't down to raw talent or mental strength. I believe it was purely down to purposeful practice and a strong curiosity about the sport. I had my role model to look up to in Andre Agassi, and all of my pocket money went into upgrading my tennis racquet to his latest version whenever it came out. We all have somebody we look up to and he was certainly it for me! My brother also got into the sport at a similar age to me and he showed a similar trajectory of improvement in his game too. He probably had more talent than I did but what did it for both of us was the purposeful practice.

Now I am not here to claim I am the first person to write about this; Malcolm Gladwell's best-selling book Outliers made famous the concept of deliberate practice. He gave the example of a famous Hungarian family whose father, Laszlo Polgar, raised his three daughters from an early age to become global chess prodigies, with Judit and Zsuzsa becoming the best and second-best player in the world. In fact, Judit is widely considered to be the greatest female chess player to have ever played the game, which shows how pure dedication and purposeful practice can lead to tremendous results. It is not about genes or raw talent to scale these heights, but rather it is about putting in the hours of consistent, purposeful practice (10,000 hours minimum to be precise according to FSU academic Anders Ericson).

My own sporting icon is Tiger Woods, who while I admit divides opinion, is without doubt the most ruthlessly focused sporting icon out there in my view and I have enormous respect for his work rate and determination to win. He is widely believed to be the first billionaire sportsman and yet he still carries the same ambition and will to win he had as a teenager trying to make it for the first time. How did he get there? Well, you guessed it, through incredible drive and determination to win. Similar to the eastern European chess family mentioned earlier, his father was infamous for his influence and obsessive efforts to make Tiger the best golfer in the world. The point is not about parenting techniques but about just what is required to be the world's best or to be an expert in a specialised field in today's cut-throat, uber competitive society. We will of course dive deeper into this subject later but for the time being the theme to take from this is that hard work, raw grit, and determination trumps perceived talent every time.

ROADMAP

One exercise I found really helpful has been purposely sitting down and creating a roadmap for what I want my life to look like. While circumstances change and plans often take a back seat, purposefully writing down how you see your life path developing is the first step to actually realising your goals. Very few people who achieve big things get there by chance and I believe the majority set out regular goals and have an overall vision of how to fulfil their potential. The following factors are important considerations along this journey:

GEOGRAPHY - The first step for me involved decided where I want to locate myself in the world. Questions to consider include whether you want to live in a warm or cool climate, have regular access to fresh salt water and beach walks or a local nature park, live down the road from your family or start anew, enjoy the hustle and bustle of city life or prefer a quiet place of reflection, home school your kids or live in a community with a strong focus on education and social activities. The answer to these questions should help you determine an ideal location for you to live, which is often the hardest question is answer.

CAREER - The next consideration involves the difficult career choices. One of the key questions to ask yourself is what kind of purpose you want to associate with and spend your time on for the next 20 to 30 years minimum. In other words, what will energise you to get out of bed in the morning and make a difference in society. Reflect on what type of skills you would like to apply in order to find purpose whether it be serving others, teaching, helping, or building. If you are really passionate about helping others then perhaps a nurse or doctor could be a great career option, teaching would naturally suit educational based industries, while building could include an aspiring entrepreneur or sales person. This internal discovery process should also focus on what you value most whether it be money and financial success (high paying professions such as accounting, doctor, lawyer), impact on society (teaching, nursing), legacy (business owner, entrepreneur), or leadership and influence over others (politician, charity, clergy) as an example. Identifying what you value and ranking these factors will help you establish your calling. The earlier you carry out this exercise the sooner you can enjoy the benefits given the small matter that many of the above-mentioned professions require years of education and qualifications as you know!

I have several friends who went down one path upon graduation only to discover they were best suited to another profession entirely and so had to re-skill themselves accordingly. However, all was not lost because to this day, many of the same friends cite their original pursuit as key to finding their true calling card. In fact, official data in the UK show that more than half of workers are planning to change career within the next five years. In the US, a recent LinkedIn survey showed that young workers switch jobs on average 4 times within the first 10 years after graduation. Overall, certain studies suggest that the average person will change career 5-7 times during their working life. Note this is a change of career and not just a change in job we are talking about!

Another important consideration is whether you can find a job allowing you to regularly work from home. This trend is increasingly common among people who value the ability to work from home a couple of days per week for the autonomy and in order to avoid commuting. Many people who have this luxury often decide to live in the countryside as they no longer have to commute for long hours every day. If you value this autonomy, make sure you check it out and do the research (the tech industry lends itself well for example). Lastly, choose an industry that will stick around during your professional lifetime. While this may sound obvious the global landscape is rapidly changing all around us and traditional industries such as car manufacturing and oil production for example may not be around in 20 years given the advancements being made with electric vehicles and alternative energy sources so plan accordingly.

SOCIAL - Social considerations are another important factor when creating your life roadmap. If you are single and looking to find the perfect match, then isolating in a remote part of the world is probably not a good idea, as it will be difficult to meet people unless you have good Wi-Fi connectivity and supreme confidence in your online dating capabilities! On the other hand, spending a couple of years in a busy city or vibrant town may help you find your match and meet like-minded people. You can start to hang out in sports clubs and exercise classes if you like the fit and sporty type, or libraries and cultural hotspots if you prefer the curious and intellectual fits. The beauty about a large city is you can boost the odds in your favour by spending time in certain places that attract your perfect match. The days of meeting people in nightclubs and bars are behind us in my view and daters are now becoming far pickier and more sophisticated. Equally, making new friends is more easily done in the sports clubs, community, and work place without the background noise of late-night bars!

HEALTH AND EXERCISE - For those who place a big emphasis on health and wellness, living by the seaside may be very important for you to enjoy a healthy morning swim and runs along the beach. Research suggests regular exposure to nature can add years onto our lives, make us happier, and reduce stress and anxiety. In addition, certain studies have shown that regularly walking on uneven terrain such as outdoor hiking can improve our wellbeing and longevity, another welcome reminder of nature's vitality and positive energy! Living in the city long term can often feel particularly unappealing for the health conscious given the pollution levels and higher health risks associated with the modern urban lifestyle. Those of us who grew up in the countryside can also find the going tough in the city bustle!

CURIOSITY

Curiosity is becoming an increasingly popular buzzword today. Billionaires from Warren Buffett and Elon Musk swear by it to achieve intense purpose and success, while certain scientists affirm that curiosity plays an important role in ageing well and keeping our mind functioning.

Equally in job interviews, how much you know is fast becoming replaced by how much you are willing to learn. Titans of industry such as Bill Gates, Jeff Bezos, and Steve Jobs are deeply curious about solving problems of the world. For example, Bill Gates is reported to have read the entire World Book Encyclopedia in his teenage years and to this day reads up to 50 books per year. Equally, Jeff Bezos unscrewed his crib with a screwdriver as a child in order to understand how the mechanics worked by rebuilding it. Another example is Steve Jobs whose former tutor described him as having a "very inquiring mind… he refused to accept automatically received truths and he wanted to examine everything himself". Elon Musk has suggested the most important soft skill he looks for in hiring candidates is a deep level of curiosity about how the world works. Buffett once remarked in an interview that he and Gates 'certainly share a curiosity about the world' and went on to confirm that this was their most important shared characteristic. Curiosity is 'an amazing thing where you try to predict what is going to happen, and then, when it doesn't, you think: Well, that drug didn't get invented, that stock didn't go up, that approach wasn't popular. What is it about my model of the world that's wrong? Who could I talk to? What could I read?', according to Gates himself.

READING

Reading is one of the best pleasures in life and is largely free of charge. Like a good bottle of wine or dark chocolate, for me it was one of those things where I gradually acquired a taste and enjoyed it more with time. I had little appreciation for reading as a teenager; my attitude was an hour spent indoors reading was another hour taken away from getting outdoors and playing sports. However, over the past 5-10 years I have gained enormous appreciation for reading and it is one of the best pastimes out there for improving your health and wellbeing. Reading not only improves our literacy as you know (given you are reading this now!), it can also improve our creativity and ideas generation as we often compare ourselves to the characters in the book without even realising it. We can also develop our personalities and habits through reading, regardless of whether we enjoy fiction or non-fiction. Think Harry Potter for example, and the millions of adults around the world who took confidence and inspiration from their childhood hero!

The great news is reading not only helps to develop our personalities and ideas, it actually boosts our health too. Despite what we may perceive to be a rather passive activity, reading can play a material role in delaying the onset of certain mental diseases such as dementia as it stimulates our mind and emotional intelligence drivers. In addition, studies have shown reading for pleasure can enhance our feelings of self-esteem and confidence in the workplace and social environment. As we have seen earlier, curiosity is a fantastic way to prolong our lifespan and there is arguably no better way to feed our curiosity than through the power of reading. As Bill Gates once remarked "My biggest problem is I stay up too late because I am reading and then I am a little bit tired the next day. This is a phenomenal time to be a curious person. The information that is out there!" His good friend and bridge partner Warren Buffett added simply, 'You can't get enough of reading'. Reading can also reduce our feeling of loneliness as we immerse ourselves in the plot of a good book. I've had this feeling myself on many occasions where I am so deep into a book on the weekend that I quickly forget about any social commitments in the diary and I'm sure you can relate to this too!

I would say the biggest benefit from reading I have experienced is the relaxed mindset and feeling of mindfulness it fosters. Reading soothes the mind and physical body, and encourages you to relax and destress from your day. Practicing 30 minutes of reading per day is like a detox experience from all the clutter and materialism in our world. It is no surprise to hear reading during this Covid-19 pandemic has increased significantly. Some estimates suggest reading time has almost doubled in the UK for the average person from approximately 3.5 hours per week to 6 hours. As many as 35% of respondents cited their primary motive for increased reading as an 'escape from the crisis'. Interestingly, certain titles such as The Plague by Albert Camus have increased sales by over 1,000% since lockdown started, while at the same time the 2006 movie Contagion has surged in viewership too as it bears a remarkably similar plot to today's unprecedented events (I highly recommend it if you haven't seen it yet!). The fact that reading has seen its popularity surge over recent months bodes well for society given the scientific backing which shows reading is associated with less loneliness, better sleep, improved relationships, and reduced symptoms of depression. It was famously said the true reason for writing is 'to enable the reader to better enjoy life, or to better endure it', and I believe this has particular relevance in today's environment. As Abraham Lincoln once quipped 'my best friend is a person who will give me a book I have not read'!

MENTORS

We all need role models, champions, and people to look up to. Whether we know these people personally is not necessarily required, although it can be helpful of course to build the trust and relationship! Mentors can give us inspiration and motivation to continue on our chosen path particularly in times of doubt. Mentors can offer us a rich supportive network to grow and develop in a safe environment, allowing us to open up about problems and challenges (i.e. a problem mentioned becomes manageable). Some studies have indicated mentor relationships can help keep young people in school, and at the same time contribute to wellbeing outcomes and engagement in the work place.

Traditionally, the mentor has always been the person in control of the relationship and often holds the key to positions of power such as promotion at work, resources, network, and opportunities. However, in recent years the mentee has begun to offer reverse mentor coaching to the mentor in order to help the typically older generation to better understand the needs of the younger cohort, and to improve their ability to interact and engage with the millennial mindset. This becomes particularly relevant when you consider the millennial generation is expected to represent over 50% of the global workforce by 2025.

Very often, this reverse mentoring approach can also help the traditional older mentor learn new skills related to technology, innovation, instant messaging, and video communication methods which can boost performance in the workplace. It is also a great way for senior management to identify talent, build relationships with the younger staff, better understand the sentiment in a company, and diversify the insights at the top regardless of demographic group or seniority.

One common mistake often made by mentees is to seek out a mentor at the very top of their game in terms of status and success. Often it can work out much better for the mentee to choose a mentor who may have more time to invest in you and may be a better fit for your particular set of circumstances. You want to find somebody who can both support and challenge your core values, and not necessarily somebody who went to the same school as you and lives in the same district. Seek out somebody different in order to find a fresh voice and new approach. Arguably the most important consideration is to find a mentor whom you can talk openly about your goals and problems. The first step in finding the right person is to identify where you want to improve, and specific areas you need help with. This takes deep self-reflection and a constructive, honest evaluation.

PERIPHERAL VISION

Having the ability to see where others can't can be a significant advantage in almost any field or profession, taking years of experience and hours of purposeful practice. Whether you work as a professional sports person, academic, investor, or medical profession, loosely defined peripheral vision or an ability to see what others can't will serve you well. For example, in one famous experiment led by the Nobel Prize winner Herbert Smith, it was demonstrated that chess grandmasters can assimilate more information from a single glance at a chess board when compared with enthusiastic chess amateurs who took 20 times as long to glean the board. The same can be said for radiologists too, who can observe much more from radiograms compared with trained amateurs.

Rugby is where I learned about the importance of peripheral vision as a teenager. Our coach spent hours training us to improve our vision around us and not to be solely focused on following the ball and field of play. More recently the England rugby team have invested in a full-time peripheral vision and hand-eye coordination expert, Sherylle Calder, who has also worked with the British Olympics team and South African rugby. She claims vision and peripheral awareness of the average person has declined significantly over the past 10 years in part due to the rise of screen-time and mobile devices. As a result, several notable high-profile coaches have explicitly advised their players to reduce screen-time to measurably improve athletic performance.

The same applies in our own life in our ability to better understand our internal feelings and the emotions of those around us. Too often we are consumed with our social media and instant messaging without realising all that is going on around us. It is only by first grasping these external influences that we can truly understand our self!

QUOTES ON SELF

'Doubt is not a pleasant condition but certainty is an absurd one' – Voltaire

'There are three things extremely hard: steel, a diamond, and to know one's self' – Benjamin Franklin

'Few are those who see with their own eyes and feel with their own hearts' – Albert Einstein

'To love oneself is the beginning of a lifelong romance' - Oscar Wilde

'Whatever you are, be a good one' – Abraham Lincoln

PART II

MIND

ILLUSORY SUPERIORITY

We are all the same. While some of us feel we are superior to others and destined for success, the reality is we all think the best of ourselves both in terms of future potential and physical appearance. Unfortunately, for the doubters among us, this is backed up by scientific research too! It is part of our human nature that we have a deeply engrained need to feel good about ourselves and we employ a number of self-enhancing techniques to achieve this. This psychological tendency is termed the 'above average effect' or the 'illusory superiority' to sound more technical, and the studies show some interesting results. For example, 85% of us rate ourselves with an ability to get on well with others, over 90% of college professors claim to do above average work, 70% consider ourselves above average leaders, and close to 95% consider themselves possessed with superior driving skills which is quite a dangerous thought! Interestingly, there is no material gender difference and statistically it goes without saying these results cannot add up.

Other related studies have shown we have a remarkably accurate ability to predict how others would behave in a certain situation, but self-enhance how we would actually behave in the same situation. For example, people overestimate how much money they would donate to charity in a certain situation, but estimate with remarkable accuracy how much other people would donate under the same circumstances. Similar results were found in other situations such as people estimate they are less likely to pick up the flu compared to others, more likely to pick winning stock investments compared with the average investor, and despite all of this evidence, the majority of us don't believe these self-enhancement bias apply to us! One great example of this is football referees who are often subjected to huge abuse from passionate fans critical of their every decision. Studies have shown referees have a unique ability to externalise stress and blame any questions about their decision making on peoples' inherent bias to a certain team or their lack of understanding of the laws, rather than internalising the decision on themselves. Not surprisingly, each referee also rates their ability higher when compared with their own peer group, underpinning the theme that no industry group is immune to this fascinating disposition! It is a classic case of while knowledge is a dangerous thing, no knowledge at all is even worse!

All of this can lead to questionable social behaviour too. Any kind of rejection on the sports field, in business, or politics, can often leave the recipient feeling hard done by. A common response is, 'how can my manager not see how amazing I am?' It affects all aspects of society and every profession in so many negative ways. We start to feel victimised and believe the person who dropped us from the team, or overlooked us for the top job acted in ill-faith and was out to get us from the start. Given we genuinely believe we are better than almost everybody else in our team or organisation, it is natural to feel this way, however knowing this psychological disposition can help us in future to think more rationally about it and ultimately reframe an initial negative outcome into a positive.

Life would be so much easier for all of us if we can face up to the fact that the vast majority of us are very normal on most reference points. Your sports ability, intelligence, career, health, romantic partners, and family home are all likely to be normal, and not exceptional as our mind often leads us to believe. Convincing yourself you are less normal and either more amazing or more miserable than the average only leads you further astray and channels more feelings of negative emotion.

BEHAVIOURAL ECONOMICS

This is a big personal passion of mine which I believe affects all of us in so many ways we don't even realise. I have read many books on the topic, and found understanding how our behavioural framework operates can have a profound impact on our day to day outlook and approach to life. Over the next few pages, I want to share several key examples of how external factors can influence our behavioural mindset, often without our awareness. For example, we live in a very materialistic world, and when you take a look at the largest global companies today, it is no surprise many of them are luxury good retailers. These are products we desire and dream about, made more exclusive by the branding and marketing strategies employed by these corporations to great effect, and who are in turn applying many of the simple behavioural tools we will discuss to feed this air of exclusivity.

THE FRUIT BOWL

Starting simply with the fruit bowl, did you know an orange is the most likely everyday fruit to be left behind. This may surprise you as most people would agree oranges are delicious and we all enjoy the taste and health benefits of eating them. However, the reason it gets left behind in the bowl is because it is one of the more difficult fruits to eat. Peeling off the orange skin is both tedious and always quite a messy process. As a result, we train our brain to avoid the orange as we associate extra effort and cleaning involved. Perhaps knowing this trick will help us to overcome this mental block and enjoy their health benefits next time we walk past the fruit bowl!

SOCIAL PRIMING

If you google 'holding a warm cup of coffee can' you will find dozens of search results all related to social priming. Social priming refers to how subtle cues can impact human thoughts and emotions and this warm drink experiment is a great illustration. Conducted by John Bargh at Yale University, he found having a warm drink in hand such as tea or coffee can influence your impression of other people and actually make you feel socially closer to those around you. Professor Bargh and his team created a way to have a group of undergraduate participants hold either a warm or cold drink in hand and then rate an individual subject. The results found students with a warm drink in hand rated the subject higher on factors related to warmth, caring, and giving compared with the students with a cold drink. Whether it be a job interview, a first date, or even meeting with a family member, numerous similar experiments have shown having a morning coffee in hand can psychologically impact how you feel about the person sitting opposite you. So next time you meet your boss for a monthly review, make sure you bring with you her preferred morning coffee fix or even better, try to schedule the meeting over a warm drink to start with! Other social priming experiments show our physical distance between people in a certain situation can impact our social judgements about another person, while you are more likely to live in a city or work in a profession with the same first letter as your first or surname. For example, Lisa is more likely to live in London and become a lawyer, while Sarah may be drawn towards Singapore and work in sales!

SNAP

Believe it or not, we tend to like people more who look like us or have a similar background. Various behavioural science research findings have repeatedly shown we hire people who went to our same school, and we prefer to hang out with people who support the same football team, wear the same clothes, or sound similar to us. These inherent human behaviour preferences are really quite dangerous particularly in today's world of equality and diverse opportunity. It is no wonder the world is so imbalanced when these inherent biases exist in our society. This also extends to the fact that similar people tend to live in the same community, hence the phrase birds of a feather flock together! Take the US for example, where a disproportionate number of billionaires live in Seattle, movie stars and celebrities flock to California, and golf stars reside in Florida.

MIRROR, MIRROR

A simple tool to stack the odds in your favour when interviewing for a job or out on a first date is to copy the other person's body language. By employing this strategy, you are improving the chances the person sat opposite will like you more, based on the behavioural research studies. Now of course this must be done in a subtle manner in order to avoid being pulled up on it, however gently reflecting their manner and posture may gradually help your case when done on a consistent basis. As discussed earlier, people like others who look and speak the same, and so the same logic applies to hand gestures and body language too!

TWO EARS, ONE MOUTH

An interesting human behaviour experiment showed we like people more who listen to us. When we are able to give our opinion and talk about our own problems to a friend or even a stranger, we tend to rate the person listening as more likeable and trustworthy than somebody who likes to hear their own voice. As the saying goes, 'you have two ears and one mouth use them accordingly', and I think we can all agree there are certain situations where it definitely pays to listen carefully and keep your mouth shut! This can also translate into the workplace or dating scene where you can stack the odds neatly in your favour without even opening your mouth!

THE MARSHMALLOW TEST

The marshmallow test (there is a book by the same name) was a really interesting experiment conducted in Stanford university in the 1960s by Walter Mischel. This experiment tasked young kids aged 3-5 years old to sit in a room with a marshmallow sitting in front of them which they could choose to either eat right away, or wait 10 minutes and receive a second marshmallow as a treat for delaying their gratification. It's one thing for an adult to be able to do this, but for a young child to have this sense of impulse control is quite extraordinary in my opinion. The study conducted this research over many years with many of the videos now posted on YouTube which I would highly recommend watching. The experiment then tracked the performance of these kids over the following decades and the results were quite staggering. Those kids who chose to exercise their delayed gratification and wait 10 minutes for a second marshmallow ended up with higher life success in terms of relationships, health, socio-economic background, and career. This is not to suggest one option is better than the other, merely having the ability to delay gratification at such a young age can have a positive impact over the course of one's life. For example, kids prioritising their homework after school rather than just playing video games and watching TV could make all the difference over the long term!

MINDSET

The study of the mind was made famous by psychologist Dr Carol Dweck from Stanford University for her pioneering work on understanding the fixed and growth mindset, where she gathered a group of students aged 9-12 years old and asked them to complete a series of problem-solving games. All students were subsequently told they got 80% of the questions right and praised for either their intelligence or hard work. The researchers then reported how these two distinct feedback groups felt and performed on future tasks. The study focused on their confidence post feedback and found that the mode of feedback delivery can determine performance and determination going forward, based on the idea that some of us rebound strongly after receiving constructive feedback while others struggle to overcome small setbacks.

According to Dweck's findings, the child praised for hard work will outperform as they are more motivated to continue working hard compared with the child praised for talent and intelligence who develop a fear of failure. In fact, the studies show quite conclusively the child praised for hard work subsequently moved on to do better in a follow up assignment, compared with the child praised for intelligence who struggled to move forward.

Children praised for their intelligence were more likely to choose future tasks they figured would make them look intelligent, while children praised for hard work and effort opted for tasks that would help them learn new things. Most importantly, children praised for effort did not fear failure and felt more confident moving outside their comfort zone to try new problems, safe in the knowledge that by praising their effort and hard work, the teacher gave them a trusted template of behaviour to follow into the next task.

The study categorised the child praised for hard work as having a 'growth mindset' and the child praised for intelligence as showing a 'fixed mindset'. A growth mindset is the idea that intelligence can be developed through commitment and hard work, while the fixed mindset refers to the concept that talent and intelligence are predetermined and come in fixed quantities. The fixed mindset tends to focus on outcomes and performance, while the growth mindset is much more focused on process and learning. The fixed mindset believes good performance and intelligence come naturally, while the growth mindset believe performance can be achieved through dedication and hard work. In addition, fixed mindset people are more likely to cheat and hide deficiencies, while the growth mindset don't have an issue with admitting failures and use these failures as an opportunity to develop and improve their process. The good news for those of you in the fixed mindset camp is that the growth mindset can be learned and developed over time, according to further research by Professor Blackwell and colleagues.

POSITIVITY BREEDS POSITIVITY

An interesting example of human behaviour at work is using certain words or actions to influence your behaviour. For example, if I ask you to complete a crossword puzzle where the majority of words revolve around positivity, you will likely report feeling more optimistic about the future than a person who has just completed a word puzzle with several solutions associated with sadness and depression. Clearly this can be used to your advantage the next time you are about to play a game of tennis against your friend; make sure you send him or her a negative video! Equally this would affirm why top athletes like Tiger Woods and Novak Djokovic spend so much time visualising outcomes and creating successful habits while preparing for competition; these actions serve as primers for the real deal. Tiger for example, always wears a red t-shirt on Sunday of competition week and his peers associate this colour with his success – talk about a self-defeating strategy!

AVAILABILITY BIAS

Availability bias feels like a game the mind plays on us whereby we believe information comes readily to mind is more representative than it really is. For example, there has been far too many shootings in the US linked to all kinds of terrible acts in recent years. While these are tragic events for all involved and everything in our power should be done to avoid such disasters from happening in future, these outbursts are still quite infrequent on a relative basis. However, when the general public is asked to rank the most common causes of death in the country, gun violence is always over represented partially because we frequently read about these tragedies on the front page of the newspaper. The surprising fact is swimming pool deaths rank higher than gun shootings in the US. Equally road traffic fatalities are far more common than aviation fatalities however it is generally the airplane accidents that make the headlines, which prompts our availability bias to kick into action and overestimate the aviation fatalities. Another often cited example is whether the letter 'k' is more commonly found as the first or third letter in a word.

We instinctively believe 'k' is more often found as a first letter because it is easier for our mind to think of words starting with 'k'. However, in reality it is found at least twice as often in a typical text as a third letter.

BYSTANDER EFFECT

Another interesting phenomenon of human behaviour is the bystander effect which explains the theory that people are less likely to offer help when they are with a group compared with when they are alone. Despite the old adage of safety in numbers, the studies demonstrate when it comes to people in need of help, the less people around the better. One clever study conducted in the aftermath of the infamous Kitty Genovese street murder in 1964, showed participants alone in a room were much more likely to report a suspicious incident, compared with a group of people left in the same room. In the simulation, 75% of participants reported an incident where smoke started appearing under a door when they were alone in the room, compared with only 10% when a group of people witnessed the same circumstances. Translating this into our own lives, when you see a person in the street drop to the pavement in need of help, don't take it for granted somebody else will call the ambulance; use your gut instinct to take ownership of the situation before it's too late. Ironically, the more people who witness the incident and walk past the person crying for help, the less likely anyone will actually help out according to the research. Reflecting on this deeper, people have a tendency to think if somebody else witnessed the event then they can help out and you can continue shopping. This is a really unfortunate state of affairs but the sooner we know about this bias, the sooner we can take it on board and react accordingly the next time we see somebody in need of our assistance. Less is more when it comes to bystanders!

ROLE PLAY

For those of you who like watching movies and dream of becoming the next superstar, it may be possible according to the behavioural scientists. In one such famous experiment at Stanford University involving a fake jail, a group of students were chosen at random by a coin flip and asked to play the character of prison guards and prisoners. Within 24 hours of the experiment's start, the guards began humiliating and abusing the prisoners, while the prisoners became timid and submissive. In fact, the behaviour of the subjects became so extreme that the experiment was terminated after just 6 days of the intended two-week period. To many, this experiment underpins why regular people, when given small amounts of power, can transform into aggressive tyrants. One clear takeaway for me is that our environment can encourage us to behave in a certain way, and that perhaps acting more assured in the lead up to an important meeting can help us to appear more confident during the crunch time!

THE BEN FRANKLIN EFFECT

Surprisingly, you can actually improve the chances of someone liking you by asking them to do you a favour! While it may seem more intuitive for the opposite to be true, the research shows that asking somebody to do you a favour builds the relationship and makes them more invested in you. Make sure you provide a reason for the favour as this boosts the chances of them accepting your request further, according to Robert Cialdini in his landmark book Influence. In addition, people who receive a favour value it most right away and less over time, while people giving the favour experience the opposite value effect. Clearly, it is important to exercise moderation as regularly asking the same people for a favour with no return for them may lead to the opposite emotions coming to pass! In his biography, Ben Franklin pondered a political man he could not win over no matter how much kindness he showed. Franklin subsequently tried the opposite tactics and it worked:

"Having heard that he had in his library a certain very scarce and curious book, I wrote a note to him expressing my desire of perusing that book and requesting he would do me the favour of lending it to me for a few days".

"He sent it to me immediately – and I returned it in about a week with another note expressing strongly my sense of the favour. When we next met in the House, he spoke to me (which he had never done before), and with great civility. And he ever afterward manifested a readiness to serve me on all occasions, so that we became great friends, and our friendship continued to his death".

This is another instance of the truth of an old maxim I had learned, which says, 'He that has once done you a kindness will be more ready to do you another than he whom you yourself have obliged'.

LOST AND FOUND

What do you do if you find a wallet on the street with lots of money inside? Professor Richard Wiseman and his team at the University of Hertfordshire decided to find out by placing over 200 wallets around the city of Edinburgh. They inserted a picture of a 'loved one' in each wallet such as a small puppy, a cute baby, a spouse, or older parents and found that almost 90% of wallets were subsequently returned when a picture of the small baby was inserted. This compared with over 50% of wallets returned with a puppy picture inside, close to 45% with a family portrait, and just 15% with no picture. If these results aren't enough to incentivise you to keep a picture inside, another double benefit of having memories of loved ones close-by is that it reduces the chances of infidelity and improves your relationship quality. For example, using the pen or cufflinks you received for your 10th wedding anniversary can be a strong reminder of your other half throughout the day.

HERD MENTALITY

Certain research suggests we can improve our communication skills by framing our message in a certain way. Studies by Richard Thaler and Cass Sunstein at the Behavioural Insights Team, have demonstrated that personalising a message significantly improves its delivery response. They sent messages to a large group of people who had not paid their court fines on time, and found clear evidence that a personalised message to include the recipient's name, was far more likely to receive a subsequent payment within the deadline, compared with a bailiff threat or other aggressive actions. Specifically, the personalised text message received a 33% payment rate when compared to no message at all, which had only a 5% payment rate. Also, advising people they are in the minority on something is a great communication tool to nudge behaviour. For example, if you are trying to crack down on customers yet to pay, informing them that everybody else has already paid and that they are in the minority will almost certainly encourage the person to settle their bill. People don't like being the odd one out, so they often feel obligated to do the same as others, even at their own expense!

ENDOWMENT EFFECT

Another funny way the mind works on the average person is it puts a strong emphasis on possessions you already own in what's known as the endowment effect. According to the Nobel Prize winning economist Daniel Kahneman, the reason is due to loss aversion, the fact we place a premium on goods we own compared to identical other goods. For example, in a famous experiment under acclaimed professor and author Richard Thaler from Cornell University back in the 1990s, half the students were given coffee mugs. Each cup was identical with precisely the same monetary value of $6 in the university shop. When the students were subsequently asked to value the mugs, the students who were given a mug valued it at $5.25 compared to the students without a mug who values it closer to $2.50. Another example relates to a wine study where bottles were bought for $10 many years ago and now worth $200 at auction. However, the owners when asked to trade their stock would neither sell the wine nor buy additional bottles at the new price. Translate this endowment effect into property, stocks, and shares and you can see how difficult it can be to reach a fair agreement for both parties!

ANCHOR EFFECT

If I was to cite one human behaviour insight I have applied most in my daily life it would be the anchor effect. The anchoring effect is a cognitive bias whereby people rely too heavily on an initial piece of information put forward. For example, if your friend estimates a bath tub full of jelly beans has 10,000 beans inside, it is more likely you will guess something close to the initial estimate put forward. One famous example of the anchoring effect involved a group of German judges who were asked to read a description of a woman caught shoplifting and then rolled a pair of dice marked with either a 3 or a 9. On average, the judges who rolled a 9 sentenced the woman to 8 months in prison, while the judges who rolled a 3 sentenced the woman to 5 months in prison, showing an anchoring effect as high as 50%! In a more practical way, when you are bidding on a property and the asking price is £300,000 your initial bid will likely be based off this number regardless of the fundamental valuation of the property because the seller has attached this anchor. Now where this can get quite expensive is when the seller is massively overvaluing the property and your subconscious mind automatically counters based on the over-priced asking price to start with. This is the anchoring effect and it is likely you encounter it on a daily basis whether you are consciously aware of it or not!

ATTRIBUTION THEORY

Attribution theory is concerned with how we explain the causes of behaviour and actions. Humans have a natural tendency to put fault on others for their failures, but cite external factors when the same outcome happens to them. Why is it when we lose our keys, we put it down to bad luck but when others lose their keys, we often accuse them of being clumsy? Other common excuses include that we fail the exam because the questions were poorly phrased, or we flunk the job interview because we weren't really interested in the job to start with. The theory of attribution all comes down to our psychological need to blame people for what happens to us. Society is full of everyday stereotypes of the attribution theory where we often suggest 'Asians are great at Math', 'Blondes are stupid', 'Americans are fat' among many, many others. These generalisations often have no factual grounding and are simply examples of our psychological bias seeking out reason to a situation.

Another great example of the attribution theory is when corporate CEOs cite their financial acumen, foresight, and leadership as reasons for their great financial performance in a good year, whereas poor performance is blamed on external factors such as the wider economic environment in a down year. A useful experiment conducted by Professor Darley and colleagues at Princeton involved a group of theology students (people we assume are particularly kind and considerate!), who were asked at short notice to give a sermon in a building across campus.

Some of the students were told they had plenty of time to get there, while others were advised they were already late. On route, each of the seminarians passed a coughing, begging man in need of help and medical attention. Close to 70% of the students in no rush offered to help the man, compared with just 10% of students already late. When we reflect on this experiment, we automatically consider the students who stopped to help the man as more considerate, despite the external time pressures clearly influencing their decision. In fact, when the experiment was subsequently described to people, the majority did not believe such time constraints would have any impact on their decision to help the man in need. As a result, most people perceived this failure to offer help as due to poor character on the part of the seminarian rather than the situation at hand!

Time and time again, we unfairly misrepresent certain groups, we hire people who are not fit for the role, we avoid people who are kind, and we put confidence in people who don't deserve it – all due to self-serving motives behind such attributions and a failure to read the wider situation. When we are running late for a meeting, we blame the train timetable, while we see others running late as disrespectful and poor time-keepers. If we are unemployed, we praise the effort we are putting in to find a job, while we see others without work as lazy and incompetent. In other words, we assign external factors to our own behaviours, and internalise motives for others – the poor people are poor because they make bad choices, while the rich are rich because they inherited their wealth.

If, however I am poor, it's because of an unfair, broken system!

One unforgettable personal example I have is from a visit to Portugal back in 2012 in the aftermath of the financial crisis. I was playing golf with some friends and we were waiting to tee-off on the first hole. Ahead of us were a group of Greeks on the fairway, and a Frenchman next in line to tee-off, waiting for the Greeks to move on. The Greeks were quite relaxed and not very good golfers. They were spraying the ball left and right, leaving the Frenchman increasingly agitated. Finally, after one of the Greeks hit another bad shot, the Frenchman started shouting at them from the tee, insisting they move to one side and let him play through. After their initial refusal, he began to slate the Greek economy and their need for a bailout from the stronger Eurozone countries such as France and Germany. He began calling the Greeks lazy, incompetent, and an unemployed wasteland. In other words, he was clearly introducing the attribution theory without even realising - needless to say, we didn't let him know there was a group of Irishmen playing behind him!

FINAL WORD

On a final note try out this very famous problem which emphasizes how our mind can lead us astray at times: If a baseball and bat costs $1.10 combined, and the bat costs $1.00 more than the ball, how much does the ball cost? Take a moment to think about this. The most popular answer is for your mind to quickly jump to the conclusion the ball must cost $0.10 however when you take a step back and allow your mind to properly reflect on the question, you realise the answer is actually $0.05 in order to ensure that the bat costs $1.00 more than the ball at $1.05 and both sum to $1.10. I have tricked many of my smartest friends with this question and I hope you have fun with it too and more importantly, remember the key takeaway!

QUOTES ON MIND

'All problems are an illusion of the mind' - Eckhart Tolle

'It is the mark of an educated mind to be able to entertain a thought without accepting it' – Aristotle

'When in doubt, don't' – Benjamin Franklin

'For there is nothing either good or bad, but thinking makes it so' – William Shakespeare

'You can't get away from yourself by moving from one place to another' – Ernest Hemmingway

PART III

HABITS

FIND WHAT WORKS FOR YOU

Routine is so important. While many of us try to emulate our role model or favourite celebrity in terms of copying their daily routine, most of us quickly fail to keep up because let's face it, no two routines will work the same for different people. We have to listen to our bodies and tailor a specific routine to work for us. While Barack Obama is known to be a night owl, staying up until after midnight to write, read, and hold conference calls with staff, Apple CEO Tim Cook prefers to rise at 4am to get to the gym. Each of us work differently and we can all achieve our goals without having to exhaust our body by adapting somebody else's daily routine that doesn't agree with us. I have plenty of good friends who are simply not morning people. They are among my smartest and highest achieving friends without question, but ask them to meet you at 6am for a workout and you will quickly be told where to go! Equally, Matthew McConaughey is known to enjoy 9-10 hours of sleep every night and this clearly works for him!

Many self-improvement studies recommend we regularly question our life direction, career purpose, and family aspirations in order to ensure we are on the right track and fulfilling our potential. Benjamin Franklin, one of my own role models (through reading) for what it's worth and among the best biographies I have read, is said to have asked himself every evening before bed 'what good have I done today?' While this may be on the extreme end, the practice of regular self-reflection can play an important role in our quest for self-improvement. Winston Churchill and Franklin Roosevelt had an evening ritual of drinks and cigars to reflect on progress and set objectives, with FDR calling it 'cocktail hour' and Churchill taking it slightly more seriously both in terms of liquor consumed and duration! Arianna Huffington and Sheryl Sandberg reportedly turn their phones off at night to limit distractions and get in the zone of connecting with oneself. Other popular techniques include journaling, to-do lists, gratitude notes, prayer, and meditation as we will discuss later.

Personally, I am a big believer in the power of the morning routine. I find it energises me and sets me up for a day of positivity. Whether it be brushing your teeth while doing 10 squats, getting out for a dawn run or row, preparing a hearty bowl of porridge with berries, or reading a book and updating your journal, these routines give me a purpose to the morning at a time when most are still in bed which I find quite motivating. Structure creates discipline and focus in my life and it all starts with the first couple of purposeful waking hours to set the tone!

THE TO-DO LIST

So many of us struggle to get our work done in a given day and feel under-resourced and stressed about the prospect of getting started on our latest task. At the same time, many of us don't even know where to start and that's where the concept of a to-do list can come in really effective. A to-do list is said to go back centuries (some credit Leonardo Da Vinci and Benjamin Franklin with creating and modernising the tool), and involves the simple task of writing down all tasks to be completed in rank order, and then crossing them off once done. Crossing them gives you satisfaction and a sense of completion and motivation to continue down the list in earnest! Many people swear by the to-do list for productivity and organisation. In addition, studies have shown a to-do list can reduce our stress and create space in our mind once written down on paper! In a similar vein to the Zeigarnik effect which demonstrates that waiters only remember orders yet to be served and quickly forget orders once completed, our mind tends to promptly forget completed tasks yet retains items still to done; another reason to keep a list!

One common issue is our struggle to tackle the larger, more intimidating items on our list. The key is to condense these big-ticket items down into more achievable bite sizes to overcome the mental block associated with larger items. For example, rather than writing down 'buy apartment', you can break it down into 'conduct viewings', 'arrange mortgage', and 'make an offer'. Otherwise, intimidating items will either get left behind and drop off the list entirely or repeatedly transfer onto your new list every week. On the flip side, remember to put down enjoyable items too like phoning a friend, date night with your other half, or researching your next holiday. Lists don't have to be all-serious and should be a combination of business, pleasure, accomplishments, wishes, and celebrations. Life should always have something for us to look forward to, and our to-do lists should be no different!

In addition, prioritise your tasks in rank order of importance, knowing that once the main tasks are complete your day can be considered a success. There is nothing worse than having a list of 20 outstanding tasks on your to-do list without any plan in place. Pledge to tackle the most important 3 to 5 tasks first and anything thereafter can be considered a bonus. Look at it from the Pareto principle; 20% of the tasks will bring you 80% of the way toward making progress in your goals. Constantly refresh and rewrite your to-do list on a daily or weekly basis as this habit will free up your mind, reduce your stress, improve your sleep, and bring renewed motivation by accomplishing the fresh tasks. Keep it simple, and trust in the process over time.

THE SCIENCE OF JOURNALING

Journaling is another great habit that helps to promote good health and wellbeing. There are lots of studies done which demonstrate that regularly writing about your day, relationships, feelings, and emotions not only clears your head and helps improve your sleep and anxiety, but the practice can also enhance your physical health too. Some notable famous journal keepers included Leonardo da Vinci, Winston Churchill, Charles Darwin, and more recently Richard Branson to name a few. One study conducted by researchers at the University of Arizona showed that people who practiced regular journaling after a divorce showed a sharp improvement in their ability to move on and detach themselves from the past, while also enjoying a lower heart rate and improved blood pressure.

Journaling imposes discipline and structure to your thoughts, allowing you to reduce stress and enhance your physical wellbeing. In addition, journaling allows us to relieve errands from swirling around our mind once written down, freeing up our headspace for creativity. The practice has been shown to be particularly effective in treating sleep issues, improving our ability to get a full night of sleep rather than waking up in the middle of the night concerned about a task we forgot to complete. Studies show journaling has similar benefits to the practice of mindfulness, and spending just a couple of minutes reflecting on your day can be very therapeutic. Very often, it can also be the first step to introducing a step change in your life, providing the catalyst for implementing a new habit or routine such as waking up early, eating healthy, and allocating more quality time for relaxation. Research studies show that in addition to reduced doctor visits, higher exam grades, and weight loss, committing to jot down your goals on paper improves the chances of you actually achieving these objectives compared with simply thinking or talking about it!

KEYSTONE HABITS

Journaling helps us to realise we are the author of our own life journey and that our chosen path is largely under our own control which can feel very empowering. Some of us often find there is a big gap between who we are and where we want to be. This can cause internal pressure, anxiety, and even a sense of despair. Rather than trying to make drastic changes to your life without thorough preparation, identifying a list of 'keystone habits' can be a great starting point to realising this change. Charles Duhigg in his book The Power of Habit describes keystone habits as 'small changes or habits people introduce into their routines that people unintentionally carry over into other aspects of their lives'. One example of this would be somebody who introduces exercise into their lives and soon realises they also start eating healthier and sleeping better as a by-product. Journaling is another example whereby you begin by writing one sentence per day and start to notice you become more aware of your emotions, feel more relaxed and less anxious. It can also help us to make sense of the big items in life and appreciate the little things such as your walk on the beach or current book. The beauty of keystone habits is they can spark a chain reaction of other good habits and start to change your life for the better!

RISE AND SHINE

Waking up early gives you an advantage on your day. Many people report early morning is the only time of the day where one can actually feel ahead of the game, rather than constantly feeling like you are chasing your tail. There have been lots of books written on the subject, most emphasising that the morning is naturally our most productive time of the day to get work done. Provided you are physically able to do it, there is merit to the argument in my view. Many of the familiar names who advocate rising early include Richard Branson (wakes at 5am daily), Michelle Obama (4.30am in recent years), Tim Cook (4am), and AOL CEO Tim Armstrong (4:30am) among many others. Those who do wake up early claim to leap out of bed and often use the 5-7am slot for activities such as exercise, meditation, reading, self-reflection, and family time. In addition, at least an hour before 9am is usually devoted to catching up on emails with several of these executives claiming to receive up to 500 per day. Many of the early risers tend to have one thing in common – they find life so exciting they want to rise early! Now clearly you can argue these people only get up early because they have high-powered jobs and not the other way around. However, there are known health benefits to making it a habit of yours too such as enhanced energy, reduced stress, better eating habits, and an increase in concentration levels. A couple of tips I found helpful to engrain the habit were:

1) Gradually get to the time you are aiming for. If you are currently rising at 8am and want to rise at 5am, initially set your alarm back 15 minutes every morning until you get to 5am rather than drastically changing your alarm to 5am on the first day and expecting your body clock to adjust accordingly, 2) Avoid hitting the snooze button. Try to get out of bed promptly once your alarm goes off in the morning, otherwise your mind will convince yourself to hit snooze and rest a little longer. Hitting snooze repeatedly in the morning will only lead to you feeling sluggish for the rest of the day, 3) Be consistent every day. Your rising time during the week should be the same on weekends in order to keep your body clock familiar with the routine, 4) Set a nice sleep routine. You can't expect yourself to wake up early without preparing your body for a good night's sleep. Ensure you get to bed at the same

time every evening and set a relaxing mood to support your sleep environment – we will touch on sleep tips next!

SLEEP

So much has been written about the importance of sleep in recent years. According to the science, sacrificing optimal sleep can lead to all kinds of devastating side effects from obesity and overeating, to a lack of concentration and inability to focus. Sleep can also help in terms of boosting your happiness and learning outcomes. One study by Dinges and colleagues examined the mood of a group of people divided into normal sleep hours of 7 hours per night and deprived sleep hours of 5 hours per night. As you might expect, the group who slept for 7 hours per night reported significantly better mood scores compared with the deprived sleep group. In addition, sleep can improve your physical body by reducing ailments and muscle strain. Sleep is also a great way to enhance your memory and creativity, which helps to understand why people suggest you should sleep on a big decision; sleep plays an important role in improving our cognitive function!

According to The Sleep Revolution by Ariana Huffington, one night of bad sleep can lead to the following: 1) increased hunger and tendency to overeat, 2) suboptimal physical appearance, 3) grumpy mood swings, 4) impaired brain tissue, 5) memory issues and loss of focus, 6) more likely to have an accident, and 7) a fragile immune system. In addition, more persistent sleep deprivation of less than 5 hours per night on a repeated basis can lead to the following: 1) increased risk or death and heart disease,

2) decreased sperm count, 3) diabetes, obesity, and certain cancers, and 4) quadrupling your stroke risk. While this all sounds very extreme, I think the point is clear that consistent sleep is a positive habit and can offer so many wonderful health benefits, often without the side effects of a prescription drug!

The obvious question is what is the optimal level of sleep? Without going into too much detail as each of us are wired differently, optimal sleep time ranges on average from 7 to 8 hours per night according to the science. While there are some well-known exceptions such as the late Margaret Thatcher who could reportedly survive on just 4 hours sleep per night, most people ignore the fact she often went for a daily nap to help improve her focus and concentration! Speaking of naps, Spain is well known for its daily 'siesta' ritual, and the country was recently predicted to have the longest life expectancy in the world by 2040, according to the WHO. However, the consistency and timing of your sleep is also imperative and this comes back to our discussion on routine. Personally, I try to go to bed by 9pm every night and have the same pre-sleep routine of board games, reading, and herbal tea every evening. Note there are no screens involved here and according to the scientific research, this is extremely important as screen time can impact the brain and in simple terms, postpone your ability to relax your eyes, switch off, and ultimately sleep (late evening exercise can be similar).

Additional scientific tips on improving your sleep quality include: 1) keeping lavender scents and candles by your bedside, 2) placing your mobile phone in a separate room overnight, 3) playing soothing music on low volume to help you avoid mind wandering, 4) wearing comfortable clothing to bed (or no clothing at all according to some sleep experts!), 5) maintain a small notepad by your bedside table to scribble down anything that comes to mind, and 6) we spend on average a third to half of total life on a mattress so invest in good quality bed sheets and suitable mattress in terms of size, material, firmness, and comfort where possible. One can argue this is the single most important investment you can make both from a health, wellness, and posture perspective. The other being a sturdy pair of shoes!

A final word on sleep which I feel is particularly relevant in today's busy culture. It can often be a perceived sign of strength to boast to a friend or colleague you only sleep 4-6 hours per night because you are so busy and important! This is not a good habit and will likely lead to health issues if sustained. Treat yourself with the attention and respect you deserve by prioritising your sleep preparation above all other appointments. By preparation time, I mean the hour or so needed to allow your body to relax and get ready for bed, whether it be by reading, drinking tea, or having a bath.

BE NICE

Treating other people as we would like to be treated is so important. We are placed on this earth for a relatively short time (depending on your philosophy and religious beliefs of course!), and one of the few ways we can truly make a positive contribution in our daily life is to treat others nicely. Imagine how much better our own day would be if we greet each other with a 'good morning', hold the door open for a person behind us on our morning coffee run, and help people out who are struggling. It doesn't cost us a dime and the simple practice of giving 30 seconds to 5 minutes every day can benefit us in so many ways. As I write this paragraph, we are in the midst of the Covid-19 lockdown and I think about the elderly cocooning in their homes, with many suffering complete isolation and lack of daily food supplies. The simple act of reaching out to an elderly person during this time to keep them company and their spirits high can make such a difference to their day. Unfortunately, we will not appreciate just how much it means to them until we reach that age ourselves!

The reality is many of us will ask 'what's in it for me?' Our world today values selfishness and materialism to the point that certain people fail to see any benefit in helping those less fortunate. Let me explain a couple of side benefits you may never have considered: 1) Giving and kindness make you happier too, and the science has shown this direct correlation between giving and your own reported happiness. 2) You never know how you can benefit in return. The person you help out may prove to be a great mentor or friend for you in future, sharing their years of wisdom and guidance. Equally in the jobs market, many companies now purposely leave you waiting in reception prior to interview or ask a secretary to walk you to the interview room as part of their criteria to examine how you interact with all staff, not just your potential hiring manager!

In addition, research has shown you are never more than six introductions away from any other person. With close to 7 billion people in the world, this theory of 'six degrees of separation' suggests Tiger Woods, Oprah, or the Queen are all within reach if we start connecting with others! Microsoft scientists scanned through over 30 billion messages from 180 million people around the world and found the six degrees theory to be accurate. A degree of separation is defined as a measure of social distance; for example, you are one degree away from people you know and two degrees away from people they know directly. My friends and I have often tried to test this theory out, and regularly found it took less than 6 degrees of separation to connect each other to random people! The point is this concept represents yet another reason to be nice as you never know where it could take you!

HOW WAITERS INCREASE TIPS

In the same vein, looking after our colleagues and customers has never been more important when you consider the fierce competition and substitute goods out there. The beauty is this personalisation doesn't need to be a grand gesture, it simply requires a genuine and thoughtful approach. For example, in the restaurant trade, one famous study showed simply following up after a customer has finished their meal is a powerful way to retain relationships and loyalty. As part of the study, waiters were asked to do one of three things after the customer had finished a meal; 1) present mints along with the bill, making no mention of the mints, 2) bring out a couple of mints by hand along with the bill and specifically mention the mints to the customers, and 3) bring out mints along with the bill, mention the mints, and come back again with more mints. While the first group of waiters managed to achieve an almost 5% increase in tips compared to the control group, the second group increased tips by close to 15%, while the third group managed to achieve a more than 20% increase in tips. While case 2 and 3 were very similar, case 3 added an extra layer of personalisation allowing the customers to enjoy more mints after they had finished the initial tray, and specifically mentioning to the customers they could have additional mints. While this example relates to the restaurant industry, clearly this can be applied to our everyday relationships and encounters with strangers. It was the waiters' proactive willingness to follow up post purchase and after the initial tray of mints that made the customers extra satisfied and more generous with their discretionary tips!

Another interesting lesson we can learn from restaurant waiters is by repeating a customer order aloud, customers are more generous in their tipping. According to a group of Dutch psychologists who discovered this finding, the difference can be substantial and well worth the effort of taking note. In their study, waiters who repeated their customer order received almost double the tips of the control group, and the researchers believe the reason is due to their belief that repetition by itself can create bonds and unilateral understanding between people, in addition to the customer feeling more confident on the waiter's ability to wait on them. It all boils down to the fact we enjoy the sound of our own voice! Other academically tried and tested approaches waiters can use include crouching down beside the customer as they order, smiling, and even touching the customer on occasion!

OUR SECOND BIGGEST FEAR

I began my quest to become a more competent public speaker at the beginning of 2013. As part of my list of new year resolutions, my mum suggested I try a club called Toastmasters International. I had never heard of it and decided to do some research. I discovered the club was represented in almost every city in the world and quickly found a host of clubs next to the office. Eventually I found one I liked and became a member to encourage my regular attendance. The whole idea of Toastmasters is to participate at your own pace and take part in sessions as you please. The club encourages you to fill roles ranging from time keeper and collecting votes, right the way up to MC and actually speaking on a topic either prepared or spontaneous.

As I learned early on, Toastmasters is there to serve you. According to reports, our biggest fear in life other than dying is public speaking and I quickly found out why! Think about it for a moment. Why is it people have such fear of standing up in front of a crowd? Yet, at the same time many people using social media feel comfortable posting their private life for the whole world to follow. It almost seems to be a genetic problem passed from one generation to another. A reported 75% of the world's population suffer an outright fear or degree of anxiety around public speaking. The reality is this fear has little if anything to do with actually speaking or the content of what we say, but instead is concentrated on our insecurity around the perceived reaction of our audience to what we say or how we look. We fear what others will think about us and of course this is made even worse by the social media and global interactions we share with others through a simple click of a button. I see Toastmasters as a remedy to treat this chronic problem, and the progress I saw in fellow members each week was truly incredible. Members who had never stepped foot on a podium before were closely mentored to build up their confidence and stage presence. Guests arriving for the first time were invited to enjoy the 90 minutes of informative public speaking and competition, before standing up and introducing themselves at the end of session. This encouraged a collaborative environment for people to get to know each other and use the session as a tool to improve certain parts of their speaking.

I found the motivation for people to join the club varied widely; some were looking to boost their career, others to improve confidence, and one even signed up to practice for an upcoming best man's wedding speech! Another great aspect of Toastmasters is the feedback delivery mechanism, which involves a 3-step process I still use today in the order of accommodation, recommendation, and accommodation. In other words, sandwiching two complements on either side of an area to work on. For example, complementing the speaker on their delivery and pitch, recommending more structure such as the power of three, before complementing their commanding stage presence!

My personal motivation for joining the club was to eradicate the use of 'crutch words' in my speaking style such as 'Um', 'Ah', and 'Like'. Too often I found myself using stall words in between sentences which both annoyed me personally and also took away from the delivery. I completed the 10 speeches required to become a 'competent communicator' and made some great friends along the journey, many with similar interests to me. Each speech is designed to focus on a certain predetermined competency to improve your overall speaking. For example, the first speech is called 'The Icebreaker' and provides an opportunity for the speaker to introduce and share a little personal story to the group. The following nine speeches range from focusing on stage presence, organising your speech, optimising your pitch, using vocal variety, and researching the topic. Each speech grew slightly longer from 5 minutes initially to about 12 minutes for the final speech which was a great way to gradually improve your comfort speaking in public. Famous alumni of the club include Harrison Ford and Julia Roberts to name a few, and so I felt like I was in good company!

PRIORITISE

Time management is a frequently underrated daily habit which can be so important for your credibility. Too often in my experience, friends and colleagues struggle to come up with an agreeable time to meet for coffee because their diaries are 'so busy'. Inevitably, one would suggest catching up at an obscure hour such as 6am or 10pm to squeeze it in and give the impression they are so incredibly important. This is the wrong approach in my view as it only leaves a sour taste in the recipient's mouth unless of course they are equally 'busy'! Prioritise people important to you and take control of your schedule. No wonder surveys repeatedly show increasing stress given we don't even have the time to meet for a coffee! According to the UK Health and Safety Executive, over 500,000 workers suffer from regular work-related stress, anxiety, or depression, and as a result over 12.5 million working days were lost during 2016/17. It generally builds over time rather than happening overnight; you start working longer hours, sleeping and exercising less, eating more spontaneously, becoming more irritable and prone to agitation in a drip, drip fashion. Even a lack of concentration, feeling of detachment from friends and loved ones, and a decline in energy can be a sign of impending stress.

Exercise and active movement are among the best ways to tackle stress and manage physical and mental wellbeing in my view. A landmark Colombia University study showed for working professionals over 45 years old, the average period of inactivity during their waking day was as high as 12.3 hours. The study found those who remained static for more than 13 hours of their waking day were twice as likely to die prematurely compared with those who were inactive for 11.5 hours per day. In addition, further research identified a strong correlation between overwork and cardiovascular problems, such as an irregular heartbeat and palpitations.

READING THE NEWS

I spend hours every day reading the news from various online publications and I have no doubt others do too. I often reflect on why I do this other than boredom and addiction, given most of the daily news headlines are old stories and often written with an agenda in mind. In reality one can argue I am trying to make myself feel better about myself given most headlines tend to be on the negative end of the spectrum nowadays. I guess this is no coincidence given the newspaper editors are acutely aware of this human behaviour trait and use it to their advantage to boost sales.

Assessing this further, who will ever remember what the newspaper reported on the 18th April 2020 for example? Or any other day for that matter. This morning, I see lots of local issues reported in the press along with the usual summary of political and economic issues of the day related to the European Union and Brexit. In reality nobody will remember these headlines by next week and our time would be much better spent reading a classic book or signing up for an educational course in my view!

GET IT IN WRITING

One small trick you can apply when dealing with a person you find difficult to judge (or in any important negotiation) is to ask him or her to put it down in writing or on email. I think this makes sense from an intuitive standpoint as when you think about it, a liar will never want to write something down on record and the research confirms this fact. Rather, they are happy to speak over the telephone as there is usually no record nor eye to eye contact. So next time you enter into an important negotiation, arrange to meet in person, write it down, or promptly follow up on email asking them to confirm all has been agreed. We have all been in this situation before and it makes it easier for everyone to know where they stand whether it be applying to college, putting an offer in on a property, drawing down your pension, or speaking with your bank manager.

SITUATIONAL FACTORS

Situational factors are one way we can implement some of the discussed habits to boost our wellbeing. According to Professor Painter at Cornell University, the situation we put ourselves in has a huge bearing on how we behave. For example, he conducted a study whereby a packet of sweets was left either in front of people on their desk or two metres away as they worked. The results found the consumption of these sweets increased by close to 50% for the group who had the sweets on the desk. How easy we make it for ourselves to reach for the 'cookie jar' has a huge bearing on our consumption patterns. Hence the well-known phrase 'out of sight, out of mind'; our ability to block out distractions and temptations in our day to day lives can have a big impact on our wellbeing. Another study was done on the same group of people whereby sweets were placed either on the desk in front of them, or in a desk drawer still easily accessible but out of sight. The results showed people consumed 25% less sweets when they were placed in the drawer compared with the group who had sweets the same distance away but plainly in sight on the desk. This can be applied nicely in our daily lives by keeping healthy foods such as a fruit bowel on our kitchen counters to encourage us to eat more, while at the same time hiding the chocolates!

Social media usage is another situational factor we can engineer as a habit in our favour to improve our happiness and wellbeing. Exercises such as keeping our phone out of sight while working and limiting our usage of certain websites like Facebook can have a significant impact on our overall wellbeing. Sleep quality can also be enhanced by purposefully keeping our mobile phones and laptops outside the bedroom at night and avoiding screen-time in the hour before bedtime as we discussed earlier. In addition, spending time with others who avoid their phones and social media can have a big positive impact, as seeing others on their phone only encourages us to do the same!

GOAL SETTING

Another practical tool we can apply in order to implement the above habits into our daily lives is to set specific goals and to visualise these goals in terms of how to achieve them. By goals, I don't mean a simple high level over-arching ambition of reading more books for example, but specifically which books you will read, how many pages per day, what time of day you allocate to reading, who you read with, where you spend your time reading whether in the park or bedroom, among other important considerations.

One interesting side note is that committing to achieve a goal is made easier when done with somebody else as you will both push each other to get it done, and you become almost accountable for each other. Think about it, it can be very tempting to skip a reading night when your favourite sports show is on television. However, if you have already committed to meeting a friend at a certain time, you are much more likely to skip the show and attend your meeting. In addition, we must also visualise the potential obstacles necessary to overcome in order to achieve these goals such as temptations like going out late with friends. The academic research suggests the more specific you are about your goal setting, the more likely you are to achieve your goals. Studies by Professor Klein and colleagues showed this to be true by inviting participants to take part in a hand-eye coordination test and found those who had a specific performance goal and strategy in place were far more likely to achieve their results compared with the default group!

One concept I don't personally agree with is that sharing your goals and ambitions with friends and family from the outset motivates you to achieve these objectives. This is another framework which derives from human behaviour economics and while it may work for some, I personally feel the opposite way. My issue is that from my experience, sharing your goals prematurely allows you to almost take credit and receive recognition before you even get off the ground! I have seen it time and again whereby a friend will tell me she intends to buy a house next month. Next month will roll on and she still has made no progress toward buying the house despite the fact that she already told all her friends and family about the goal. In other words, she received the credit and applause from friends and family prematurely and this was enough. The academic research suggests it is a good idea to share your goals and aspirations with others in advance as it holds you to account and motivates you further to achieve your goals. In my life I try to keep things quiet until long after the fact. Sharing achievements with others only creates friction and envy in my view. One is much better off keeping the head down and going about their business in a quiet, progressive way. When was the last time you saw one of the wealthiest people in the world brag about their latest profit, or one of the best academics boast about their latest research publication? It doesn't happen and for very good reason. Slow and steady works well.

QUOTES ON HABITS

'We are what we repeatedly do. Excellence then is not an act, but a habit' – Aristotle

'Your net worth to the world is usually determined by what remains after your bad habits are subtracted from your good ones' – Benjamin Franklin

'Quality is not an act, it's a habit' - Aristotle

'It is easier to prevent bad habits than to break them' – Benjamin Franklin

'If you think adventure is dangerous, try routine; it is lethal' – Paulo Cuelho

PART IV

FAILURE

OVERCOMING SETBACKS

There is no doubt in my mind I am a failure. Over the past 20 years I have failed exams and certain relationships, lost out on job interviews and promotions, disappointed family and loved ones due to my decisions, let down my teammates on the sports field, and lost money due to poor choices. Regardless of this long list, I am still alive writing this journal and feel happy, healthy, and positive because I have learned to look at failure in a new light, as a key stepping stone to future success. As the famed American footballer Lou Holtz said, '"Show me someone who has done something worthwhile, and I'll show you someone who has overcome adversity".

Adversity is a necessary step along the path to success and the quicker you come to terms with this, the sooner you can achieve your goals. If you don't put yourself forward to sit the exam, try out for the sports team, ask the girl out on a date, or set up your business, you will never know how your life might have turned out. According to the research, the biggest regret people have on their death bed is not taking a risk, because they feared the consequences and social stigma of failure. If this doesn't drive you to give your idea a try, then nothing will! While staying in the comfort zone may make you look good and avoid failure in the short term, the reality is you are decaying at a rapid rate and you will soon find yourself streets behind in today's uber competitive society. Rejection is part of the journey and rather than seeing a setback as a slap in the face, remember success is a probability game, the more paint you throw at the wall the more likely it is to stick, and it is the same with setbacks and failure. For what it's worth, I have been rejected for 95% of the jobs I have applied for, but now I realise in hindsight each rejection was actually a step closer to getting in the door.

Behind every successful sportsperson, business executive, or wellness guru is a long list of obstacles and challenges that could have ended their dreams. Often you reach a point on your journey where everything seems to be going against you, but then out of nowhere along comes a ray of hope (whether it be an email reply, chance meeting, or phone call) that gives you the courage to continue. It is so important to trust your gut instinct both in terms of when to persevere, but equally important, is when to cut your losses and try something different. For example, right now in the midst of Covid-19, structural changes to the transport and hospitality sectors may prove challenging headwinds to overcome and spur an aspiring start-up to pivot toward another industry. At the same time, it is important to have perspective given history suggests this crisis will spur opportunity as many of the greatest companies in the world were created during times of recession such as Toyota, Disney, HP, General Motors, and Airbnb more recently.

During these times of setback, it is really important not to beat yourself up and instead be nice to yourself. As Winston Churchill aptly put it, "success is never final, failure is never fatal, it is the courage to continue that counts". Reflect on your situation and put it into perspective as a wake-up call. Remember everyone experiences setbacks and often these setbacks can be a signal to pivot or adjust something about your business model, study technique, or training regime. Use the setback as an opportunity to go back to the drawing board, reassess your strategy, and pay attention to any advice you receive from mentors or more experienced counsel. As Thomas Edison said 'Genius is 1% inspiration and 99% perspiration' – this is your opportunity to put in the hours to understand what works and what doesn't, so use the time wisely!

One of the best ways to overcome our fear of failure is to apply a social psychology phenomenon called 'the spotlight effect', which is a term used to describe our tendency to overestimate how much people notice about us. Given the social media influence, we have a massive tendency to believe people are paying attention to our every move, despite study after study indicating this is simply not the case. Humans are selfish by nature and people are focused on themselves. The fact is nobody cares about what you are doing with your life – all the more reason to be less self-conscious and get started on making your dreams a reality. In my experience, most of my key setbacks to date have proven to be a positive in hindsight. In high school, I desperately wanted to become a lawyer, but missed out by a long shot in the academic points race despite putting in serious study hours (which only compounded the bad feeling!). I remember my uncle consoling me in the back seat of the car as I cried desperately thinking the worst, however he gave me great advise that things would work out for the best. In the end, I studied economics at my choice university and thoroughly enjoyed it to the point that in hindsight, I would do the same all over again, and at least partially as a result, I managed to work at several of the world's largest financial firms. 'Always bear in mind that your own resolution to succeed is more important than any other one thing', the wise words of Abraham Lincoln again.

DON'T BE AFRAID TO FAIL

Failure can be such an expensive lesson. For many of us with limited resolve, a failure can completely set us back from our goal and leave us depressed and lacking confidence. For others failure can be the catalyst to get back up again and try twice as hard. Michael Jordan is one of the best recent examples of overcoming failure. Believe it or not, Michael didn't even make his high school basketball team. He was devastated when the team list was posted without his name. In fact, he was reportedly ready to give up the sport at that point until his mother convinced him otherwise. Instead, he vowed to use the disappointment to scale new heights as he recalled, 'whenever I was working out and got tired and figured I ought to stop, I'd close my eyes and see that list in the locker room without my name on it, and that usually got me going again'. While for most people, public failure leads to humiliation, for Jordan it was always an opportunity to fuel the fire, 'I've missed more than 9,000 shots in my career. I've lost almost 300 games. Twenty-six times, I've been trusted to take the game-winning shot and missed. I've failed over and over and over again in my life. And that is why I succeed'. If that wasn't enough, he also inspired the next generation of players to work hard and enter the game such as Kobe, Magic, and LeBron!

Another great example of failure breeding success is the actor Steve Martin who before becoming a household actor spent years touring restaurants and comedy clubs to refine his comedy style. As he recalled, 'everything we learned in practice, and the lonely road, with no critical eyes watching, was the place to dig up my boldest, or dumbest, ideas and put them onstage'. Equally his story puts paid to the notion of an overnight success, 'I did stand-up comedy for eighteen years. Ten of those were spent learning, four years were spent refining, and four were spent in wild success'.

The point here is that in order to succeed, we must first learn to fail. Jordan is by no means on his own, as all professional athletes and high-performance professions can attest to the same principles. A good place to start is to ask why top-class figure-skaters fall over more in practice compared to average figure skaters. The reason is because top skaters put themselves in more challenging positions in practice in order to get the best out of each session. By contrast, average figure skaters stick within their comfort zone and only attempt the easy jumps they already know how to perform. As a result, the top figure skaters are constantly improving by repeatedly failing, while the average skaters may look more impressive as they stay on their feet, but the reality is by not failing, they are simply not progressing.

The truth is the vast majority of us are risk averse by nature. We like to avoid risks where possible and travel the easy path in life. We prefer to take the full-time job with a mature, established firm and solid salary rather than join the start-up with little or no salary for 6 months. Certainly, in my own case, I joined an established firm in an industry associated with high pay in order to enjoy the short-term benefits without necessarily paying attention to where I would like to be long term. At the same time, we teach our children to avoid failure and achieve success to such an extent that many parents actually punish failure and reward success without realising the damage this is causing to the child's ability to appreciate the value of failure. Failure should be celebrated as one step closer to success and ultimately, life is about failing time and time again. If you are not failing regularly you are probably not trying to expand outside your comfort zone, because in order to be successful in life, one has to take measured risk. Unfortunately, our comfort zone tends to hold us back, acting as an impediment to risk taking and pursuing goals. For those of us in this camp it is worth noting that while 'things may come to those who wait, but only the things left by those who hustle'.

Society needs to come to terms with the fact that without failure, there is no success. Without getting back up from our defeats and building our mental resilience, we will not achieve the impossible and make progress. While professional athletes know how to deal with failure as they have been educated about the link between psychology and success, the average person is still oblivious to the fact that reframing our psychology is the first step to understanding how to link failure to success. We believe for example that our intelligence is fixed, however as Professor Angela Duckworth has shown in her fantastic book Grit, academic success is more related to hard work and determination rather than genes and natural intelligence!

After all, many people admit it is only after suffering repeated failure they find success. There is arguably no greater example of overcoming failure than the creator of Harry Potter, JK Rowling, who gave hope to the rest of us in a recent Harvard University commencement speech by sharing, 'I had failed on an epic scale. An exceptionally short-lived marriage had imploded, and I was jobless, a lone parent, and as poor as it is possible to be in modern Britain, without being homeless'. She then went on to argue that failure allowed her to succeed in the one field she was passionate about, writing, and to strip away the rest. For her, 'rock-bottom became the solid foundation on which I rebuilt my life', because she did not allow the world to label her the set criteria of failure. As she put it, 'it is impossible to live without failing at something, unless you live so cautiously that you might as well not have lived at all – in which case, you fail by default'. She spent countless hours unemployed moving from one Edinburgh café to another writing her Harry Potter drafts, while at the same time receiving welfare benefits. Once she finally finished the first draft, she received rejection letter after rejection letter without any sign of hope her hard work would make it onto a book shelf. Even after hiring an agent, she subsequently received a further 12 rejections before one publisher took a chance (best decision they have ever made!). This point alone shows the importance of persistence; had she not had the determination to dust herself off, the world would be without Harry Potter. She has since gone on to become the best-selling author of all time – with over 500 million copies sold - and the world's first billionaire author!

Re-framing failure as a critical recipe for success gives us the confidence needed to reach for the stars and achieve our dreams without concern for how others perceive us. While failure can be heart-breaking, it can also be the catalyst to rethink our goals and life path for the better. For many, it takes a brush with failure to realise what's truly important. As Wayne Gretzky, the Canadian ice hockey legend often described as the best player ever, famously said 'you miss 100% of the shots you don't take'. Let this be a lesson for all of us!

IMPACT BIAS

Harvard psychologist Dan Gilbert coined the term 'impact bias' to describe our tendency to emotionally overestimate both the intensity and duration of a future event such as the happiness derived from a new job, more money, or indeed our new found romance. The interesting thing about the impact bias is that it is much worse for negative events compared to positive. Gilbert studied a host of scenarios such as asking students how they would feel if they failed an important test. He also asked faculty how they would feel if they did not achieve their university tenure. Both results found the students and faculty felt much better than they initially expected after realising they failed to reach their goals.

As you can see, humans have a strong tendency to believe negative outcomes will affect them by much more than they actually do. The fact is time really is the best healer, and that the bad break-up or failed test result really doesn't impact our wellbeing by nearly as much as we expect. We are not aware at the time just how strong our ability is to adapt and bounce back from these life setbacks. Our mind and psychological tools are so much more resilient than we realise and this can have profound impact in our day to day life. In general, society is becoming more and more risk averse. We are reluctant to apply for that left field job because we fear the rejection on the other side. We decide not to pursue the risky business opportunity with our friend because we know how few entrepreneurial start-ups actually succeed, and we automatically assume the safer option is to take the full-time job offer instead. Our mind and culture are trained to play it safe and avoid risk taking at all costs, to the extent that many of us will regret later in life we didn't reach for our full potential and take more risks when we had the opportunity.

ASSERT YOURSELF

Stress is part of our day to day lives and nobody on the planet can claim to be immune from this naturally occurring state. While certain amounts are healthy, unfortunately excessive stress can have a profoundly negative impact on our quality of life. One useful tool shared with me to overcome stress is to practice self-assertion. Assertion refers to directly respecting who you are, what you stand for, and what you do. It involves holding true to your values and not giving in to others when pressured to do something or go somewhere without your own discretion. It is taking responsibility for yourself and your actions, because if there is one certainty in life, it is that not everything will go in your favour!

Assertion also means backing yourself even when you decide to change your mind on short notice. Stay true to your values and don't allow yourself to fall into the herd mentality of following others without first understanding and forming your own judgement. For example, take time to sleep on a decision if necessary and don't be shy about letting somebody know you are not in a position to commit right now. Give yourself the time and respect you deserve to make your own mind up and form an opinion, without giving into peer pressure. Don't be afraid about the consequences of speaking up and sharing how you feel, as the flip side is far worse given you will likely live with regret. Hoping somebody else will speak up on your behalf is a recipe for disaster and should not be relied upon. Many people fear that acting assertively will lead to others thinking you are stubborn and selfish minded, while the reality is that people will respect you more for it. By speaking up for yourself, you are simply putting you own view on an equal playing field with others. Think of other people you know who are direct and assertive; most of us respect people more who aren't afraid to voice their concerns and speak their mind!

Thought biases are another tool we can use to improve assertion. In summary, the concept of thought bias is simply seeing the glass half full rather than half empty, and utilising our positive filter to shape our outlook. For example, contextualise your negative thoughts; just because you are having a bad day in work doesn't mean you are a failure in your job, it simply means you are having one bad day and can bounce-back tomorrow. Another common example is mind reading where we convince ourselves a colleague or friend is thinking negatively about us at any given moment, despite them quite likely thinking about something else entirely. Tunnel vision is similar where we focus on the negative aspects of a particular situation without seeing any positive, alternative view. For example, just because your friend arrives late to the dinner party doesn't mean they don't like you, it could simply be due to a family emergency or traffic congestion. Don't assume the worst in a situation and instead, try to contextualise and see the positive side in a balanced way. If you lose your job, don't see it as the end of the world, instead be honest with yourself and reflect on whether it was the right fit for you in the first place. In addition, ask yourself whether you were passionate about the industry and mission statement of the firm. Perhaps it is a blessing in disguise for you to lose your job so you can find something more suited to your strengths!

Avoid jumping to conclusions about an outcome and be honest with yourself upon self-reflection. Try to project forward, look for perspective, and ask yourself how you will feel rather than getting sucked into the shock and negativity of the moment. Once you have confronted yourself, focus on your breathing and incorporate mindfulness into your routine for 10 minutes per day to bring your mind into the current moment. Notice when your mind drifts into these negative thoughts and bring it back to the present through breathing. The key is to recognise early when you are thinking about negative and stressful thoughts, realise there is nothing you can do in the short term, and promptly bring yourself back to a relaxed state. Try to utilise your negative thoughts as a direct cue to bring yourself to a happy place as this will reduce your stress and improve your mood over time!

PRIORITY ONLY

Prioritising is another great way to leverage our assertion. Structure your day as you please and not how others want you to fit into their day. Manage your time and reduce external demands by limiting certain requests. Rather than going out with different friends every night of the week, try to schedule a group of friends together on the weekend to save you the time and burden. Nobody will remember whether you went out on a random Tuesday night and you are very unlikely to miss out on anything interesting for those of you with FOMO! Prioritise your time and focus on optimising your lifestyle choices such as health, diet, and exercise. One helpful tool is to organise your daily schedule into blocks to ensure all activities you want to achieve are accounted for and your role is reduced to a time-keeper, making sure you make each appointment on schedule without the added stress of running from one meeting to the next hopelessly trying to save face!

At the same time, create the space you need to prioritise your self-emotions. Often the stigma surrounding mental health and failure in the work place can encourage people to avoid signing up and dealing with it. As a result, many organisations have rebranded programs designed to manage stress in order to avoid mentioning any association with mental health such as 'Wellbeing', 'Positive Feelings', and 'Thrive' among others. In a similar way, there is a huge negative connotation traditionally associated with seeing a psychologist or psychoanalyst, despite the fact we can all benefit from the experience in order to better understand ourselves and our drivers. Too often we are happy to spend a couple of hours watching television but rarely invest 10 minutes to reflect on how we are feeling. However, I think this will change over time as we come to realise the benefits from such exercises.

SURPRISE FAILURES

Even the best of us suffer sometimes and it is by going through this suffering and coming out the other side that we become stronger and often more energised than before. Many of the greatest influencers have suffered more setbacks than you can imagine as we touched on earlier. For example, Albert Einstein couldn't speak until he was 4 and struggled to land a permanent job as an aspiring scientist well into his 30s upon graduation. Abraham Lincoln suffered with depression for most of his life despite saying as a young man he wanted nothing more than 'to link my name with something that would contribute to the interest of my fellow man'. He faced financial struggles and broke off his engagement as he felt unable to provide for his future wife. During this time, he claimed he was 'the most miserable man on earth and unable to find the will to work again'. His friends feared he could do self-harm and so removed razors, knives, and sharp items from his room. It is easy to forget Lincoln went from a man who lost 8 elections, failed in two businesses, lost his job, was rejected from law school, and suffered a nervous breakdown restricting him to bed for as long as 6 months, to arguably the most impactful US President in history.

Equally, Benjamin Franklin was another titan of society all too familiar with failure. Several of his early newspaper and publication ventures went out of business, with two failing after just 6 months. In addition, he struggled badly as a family man, after raising 3 children but only maintaining a healthy relationship with his daughter. He also left his wife for months and years on end as he travelled extensively to Europe, and wasn't even by her side when she became fatally ill. He famously remarked 'do not fear mistakes, you will know failure, continue to reach out'. Another notable quote on failure came from the acclaimed light-bulb inventor Thomas Edison who commented, 'I have not failed. I've just found 10,000 ways that won't work'. Allegedly Edison was also told by his teachers he was stupid! More recently James Dyson, the billionaire inventor, said he worked through over 5,000 failed prototypes before he landed on success, and stated each of these failures were crucial to him achieving his empire today, 'you can't develop new technology unless you test new ideas and learn when things go wrong. Failure is essential to invention'.

MID-LIFE CRISIS

We all face some kind of mid-life crisis in my view. While some manage to rebound quickly and get back on track, others take longer and go through a deep self-reflection period whether they are conscious of it or not. While the meaning of a mid-life crisis can vary, I see it as any moment (usually from your late 30s) when you start to have second thoughts about your identity, direction, and self-confidence. I read an article recently which suggested that age 31 is one of the most difficult years for most as you begin to realise you are getting into the serious fourth decade, often without having much to your name. Societal pressure means we are often expected to be in a long-term relationship, bought our first home, and advancing in a chosen career. However, in my experience and reflecting about myself, friends, and associates, the reality can be much different!

Something about the early 30s seem to open people up to the world for the first time. We start to question whether we are running out of time and on the right path in life. Invariably social gatherings with friends bring up the same questions of comparison, probing into each-others' lives to find out how relationships are going and how much money is in the bank. Age 31 seems to bring more questions than answers, more uncertainty than clarity. We all seem to enjoy the benefits of turning 30, such as landmark birthday celebrations, steady income, and recognition from family, however 31 really seems to hit us hard in terms of second guessing our life goals and direction. Perhaps I am not so special after all, maybe I won't be rich or famous, and will never find the girl of my dreams. It's a difficult period for both men and women equally. I would argue it hits the men slightly harder on the career side of things, and perhaps the women harder on the relationship side. Men ask themselves is this really my career calling, while women calculate whether to rush into the next relationship for fear of leaving it too late. For many, there is a loss of ambition at this age too; one is no longer interested in making it 'big leagues' and being defined by their work. Instead, they now want to find a purpose with more meaning – this is the quintessential millennial mindset. Finding something with purpose that can have an impact on society and leave a legacy too!

The decision about where to settle down invariably pops into discussion at this age too. Some want to retreat to the countryside and enjoy the leisurely walks on weekends, while others want to find a home in the city to reduce their daily commute. Also, on the agenda is whether to buy or rent, with many relying on the bank of mum and dad for deposits. The decision of when to buy is one that can cripple one's finances for the next decade if made at the wrong time. My generation have lived through the 2007/08 crisis when so many were caught out by the negative equity trap, finding themselves having to work double time to pay off the mortgage. It is this uncertainty and fear of failure which feeds the mid-life crisis and lack of direction in the first place as I see it.

Millennials are a generation who fear commitment of any kind and this can be clearly seen in societal trends such as the average age of a home buyer which continues to move into the mid 30s, the average age of marriage which shows a similar trend, along with the average tenure of work which demonstrates millennials jumping from one unstable job to another compared to previous generations who typically held one job for life. Overall these insecurities and life trends only lead to higher anxiety and negative emotions which are all too evident in recent health surveys which show this generation is carrying the weight of their elders in many ways! Hence, we see the unfortunate trend that the mid-life crisis happens earlier and more frequently compared with prior generations.

Possible cures to overcome the recurring mid-life crisis include taking up more meaningful work where you can see a measurable impact, volunteering to help others, reducing your commute time, spending more time with friends and family, and taking up enjoyable hobbies that help you have fun. The key to job satisfaction is to find a role that plays to your strengths, a role where you feel like you can really contribute. In addition, finding a state of 'flow' on the job is something that really helps your job satisfaction. Professor Martin Seligman, best-selling author of Authentic Happiness and 'father of positive psychology', has coined this idea of matching your strengths with achieving flow on the job to find your optimal state of performance. By flow, he refers to finding a challenging job that suits your skillset and immerses your focus to the point that you lose track of awareness. Flow is often discussed on the sports field and music arena where top performers often cite their peak performance coming in times of a flow state similar to being 'in the zone'. The vast majority of us have experienced a flow state in our life to date, and some experts believe the best moments in our lives actually occur when we are stretched to capacity to achieve something challenging yet rewarding, a task that is difficult to achieve but still attainable through hard-work.

CRISIS COHORT

Millennials who graduated between 2008-11 are now being termed the 'crisis cohort' because we wear the scars of the global financial crisis to some extent. We joined the work force at a time of few jobs and large salary cuts. As a result, we have become accustomed to fewer hours, inferior pension benefits, and less job security. In fact, the under 30s today are almost 50% more likely to be working fewer hours, and close to 70% more likely to be made unemployed when compared to the more senior, expensive colleagues (according to government data). This goes some way to explain why millennials report disproportionate mental health issues and depression. However, on the positive side despite all of these challenges, it is the young people who are more ethically and morally driven compared to older generations, inclined to practice a vegetarian diet, more conscious of the carbon footprint and recycling efforts, and determined to make a positive social impact on the world. At the same time, this is the generation who value experiences over material possessions, no longer craving the latest fashion accessory and instead preferring to go for a hike in the mountains or walk along the beach to celebrate a birthday or special occasion.

RELEASING THE SHACKLES

Too often, it's the people who rise to the top of their chosen career path whether it be finance or medicine, before realising upon self-reflection they no longer feel fulfilled. Despite having more money and health than most could dream of, they somehow feel empty inside and want to find another pursuit to meet their need for purpose in retirement. It's the people who find the courage to abandon their initial career for the benefit of what society asks of them who are the truly courageous ones in my view. The world celebrates individual achievement however it is really the feeling of being part of a collective, bigger picture that leads to happiness and belonging. The current Covid-19 pandemic may serve as a timely catalyst to shift this dynamic as there has been lots of focus on the bravery of frontline medical staff around the world who have shunned the spotlight to help battle the virus and save lives. In fact, I think it is fair to say that without their expertise and courage, the world would be in a much worse state. Society may change how we value people and contributions after this pandemic and so we should. The days of celebrating and rewarding ego and individualism should be banished and replaced by recognising and acknowledging the power of unity. At the end of the day, we all go through life together and we feel much more engaged and happier when we are sharing our lives with others. Embracing society whether as a volunteer or getting involved in community clubs is a sure way to build appreciation for others, while at the same time feeling more fulfilled and grateful as part of a wider collective.

QUOTES ON FAILURE

'Whether you think you can or you can't, your right' – Henry Ford

'It takes many good deeds to build a good reputation, and only one bad one to lose it – Benjamin Franklin

'When you reach the end of your rope, tie a knot and hang on' – Abraham Lincoln

'The best way to predict your future is to create it' – Abraham Lincoln

'You should never think about the negatives. I didn't. I always looked at competition winning putts as an opportunity, never as a threat' - Jack Nicklaus

PART V

HEALTH

NATURE

Getting out into nature can be so transformative for one's health and is a great example of the old saying, 'the best things in life are free'. From walking on beaches and swimming in the sea, to hiking in the mountains and watching the sun go down, all of these incredible activities are generally available without a queue, subscription fee, or an annoying waiting list! While many of us still attach huge status to the latest iPhone or accessory, the older generation have long looked past these material possessions and focus almost exclusively on the memories and simple pleasures of life. My personal favourite is swimming in the sea, I absolutely love the fresh salt water and waves hitting my face while my feet touch against the sand. When swimming in the sea, I can finally stop thinking about work or other concerns, and enjoy one of life's simple pleasures, while at the same time boosting my skin health too!

LONGEVITY

We all want to age well and enjoy our twilight years with an active lifestyle. For many of us, we have spent a lifetime working and are ready to finally enjoy the fruits of our labour with family and close friends. At least this is our hope. However, the reality can be quite different with many placed into care homes with little social support or companionship on offer. In fact, isolation, depression, and detachment can be common complaints of people who are put into a nursing home partially due to the sad fact that they are often there against their will. For anyone who has had a loved one in a residential home, you will know how expensive they can be and that residents have little choice over their daily meals, who they interact with, and how they spend their time.

This epidemic of isolation and loneliness is an area 'positive psychology' has been working to improve with a recent German experiment showing inter-generational housing can play an important role in improving the lives of all generations, including the kindergarten and the elderly alike! In fact, Germany appears to be the world leader in realising the benefits of inter-generational networks to improve the quality of life for all. Buildings across the country now house a kindergarten, a social centre for the elderly, and middle-aged coffee rooms all under one roof to encourage inter-generational interactions. You may wonder how the elderly can help the kids, or how the teenagers can benefit the grandparents but the answer is surprisingly simple. Teenagers can show the elderly how to work the internet and mobile phone, along with providing companionship, while at the same time the elderly can relieve parents of their duties to look after the kids for a couple of hours, often educating and providing wisdom at the same time.

When you consider the rapidly rising cost of childcare and ageing demographics across the world, all of a sudden this seems like a great idea and a win-win for society as a whole. Giving the elderly more autonomy, responsibility, and decision-making choices can have a material positive impact on their wellbeing and longevity according to several well publicised studies. These health benefits can then free-up much needed capacity in our public hospitals and at the same time make available money and resources for the government to spend elsewhere. The simple art of keeping the elderly stimulated, purposeful, and engaged with others can improve their physical and mental health, reduce the probability of disease, and enrich life satisfaction levels. Studies have shown increased social interaction is linked to reduced risk of disease, lower incidence of hospital admission, and even improved diet, hydration, and physical exercise. In addition, increasing the elderly's exposure to young children has been shown to improve their memory capacity and reported mood!

A now famous study was created to examine the impact of giving a sense of control and responsibility to the elderly in residential homes by splitting over 90 participants into 3 groups. The first group were told by the director that everyone had significant responsibility for their own lives, and could choose any two nights of the week to enjoy a movie night, while at the same time trusted with responsibility to care for a plant left in their bedroom. The second group were given the same direction however any reference to responsibility or control was omitted so they were given the two evenings they could enjoy a movie night, and they were told a plant left in their rooms would be nurtured and fed by a nurse. The third and final group were not given any specific instructions and were left to their own devices. Each of the

90 odd participants were monitored over the proceeding 18 months at regular intervals for a range of measures including activity levels, health, sociability, mood, and mental stimulation. As you might have guessed, the first group who were given responsibility showed the greatest increase in life satisfaction and longevity, strongly demonstrating the positive effects of autonomy.

In terms of our everyday life, there are a number of tools we can apply in order to boost our longevity. Given we now know through science that feelings of social connection and community go a long way toward boosting our wellbeing and human connection, increasing our everyday interactions can have a material impact on our longevity. For example, striking up a conversation with fellow passengers on your commute to work, or peering into somebody's shopping basket in the supermarket store to ask about the cookies they picked up is an easy way to interact! It is through these daily moments of spontaneous interaction we can feel happier and live longer according to the studies. In addition, forming new habits that stimulate our mental and physical memory such as crossword puzzles, card games, and board games are great ways to age well! My own grandmother is a great example, as she is among the most active people I know, reading the daily newspaper, completing the daily crossword, and playing bridge up to 5 times per week. In fact, she also follows the daily stock and commodity markets better than most professional investment managers in my view! She is a remarkable woman and without doubt one of my most inspiring role models.

AGE PRIMING

There is lots of scientific research showing we excel at certain skills during certain periods in our life. For example, it is easiest to learn a second language when we are under the age of 10, while brain teasers are reportedly best answered by 18-year-olds, suggesting to some experts this age may be our most active brain processing stage. Another study demonstrates we are best able to remember certain short-term events in our early 20s, such as the name of a person we just met. At the same time, we are physically strongest in terms of our muscle health and bone density in our 20s, as our muscle mass and bone density start to decline quite quickly after hitting 30. Our personality also changes more in our 20s than during any other decade. While many would suggest our 20s is a time of exploration and finding ourselves, on the contrary this is the time for setting a strong foundation. For example, the money we earn in our 20s in many ways determines the money we earn in our 30s and beyond. So, landing that strong job early can really pay dividends longer term!

Elsewhere, surveys on wellbeing suggest our highest reported life satisfaction is in our early 20s and late 60s. In addition, 26 is the magic number for those looking to settle down in a relationship, while marriages are reportedly most durable when couples tie the knot between the ages of 28 and 32. Don't lose hope if you are above this age however, as another study showed most Nobel Prizes are won at age 40, and the same study showed people tend to do their best work in middle age. Salaries also tend to peak in middle age, around age 40 for women and closer to 50 for men. As a side note, a telling study on loneliness conducted by Brunel University showed that 40% of people aged 16-24 years old reported feeling lonely on a regular basis compared with just 27% of people over age 75. While the younger group may have had many more online Facebook friends compared with the older cohort, these friendships were not quality relationships where you can pick up the phone and meet up for a coffee!

Emotional intelligence is also said to peak in middle age. Interestingly for older folks, studies show we most enjoy our body confidence and physical appearance in our late 60s, and not in our early 20s as you would imagine given we are in peak physical condition around this time! On the contrary, it is our self-love and respect that drives this comfort in our late 60s rather than our gym endurance. In addition, it's the cohort in their 80s who report the most psychological wellbeing which implies they best understand their meaning and life purpose.

In preparing this book, a lot of people in their 50s and 60s told me they have never felt so comfortable and confident in their own skin, without a care in the world for how other people perceive them! Life is here to be enjoyed and the sooner we can come to terms with our own emotions, the earlier we can accept our imperfections and limitations. In my view, life is all about making the most of the little things, as once we get older and start to reflect, we realise the little things were in fact the big things! The survey results also show we like to make our big decisions in life just before we hit our next round number such as 30 or 40. For example, this is the time when we are most likely to buy a flat, get married, and run a marathon according to the studies. Taking this marathon finding a step further, studies suggest the most likely age to run a first marathon is age 29, while the second most likely age to run a first marathon is age 39!

The list of expected achievements for those turning 30 often include a long-term relationship or marriage, buying a house, and promotions at work. We tend to treat life as a laundry list of items to accomplish by a certain age, and miss the wider purpose of why we are here in the first place! Our 20s, widely known for making stupid mistakes, is often considered as the defining decade for several reasons:

1) 80% of life's most important moments usually take place by the age of 30,

2) close to 70% of life-time wage growth happens during the first career decade,

3) over 50% meet our better half in our 20s whether or not we act on it then or reconnect later!

THE MAGIC PILL

Based on all of the above findings, if you had a pill that could stop biological ageing, at what age would you choose to take it? This is the question many of the leading longevity experts have been asking as they continue making great progress toward extending lifespan. Interestingly, their answer depends on what age you are now. For example, if you are currently in your 20s, you will likely believe that 30 or 40 is too old and therefore choose to swallow the pill in your 20s. However, if you are currently in your 80s or 90s, you will likely choose to take the pill in your 40s or 50s after the kids have grown up and you have one eye on retirement. Contrary to what you may expect, there is no right or wrong answer here and your situation is deeply personal. Some believe the best age is when their opportunities are greatest, compared to others who prefer to hit pause in their 60s or 70s at peak life satisfaction. Interestingly, the late 60s and early 70s is the period when people report having the most fun and time affluence, while the least fun time is reported to be around your mid to late 30s according to studies. For what it's worth, combining the survey results and adjusting for sex, people choose 50 years old as the perfect age for living. At this age, you begin to realise how short life really is and how fortunate you are to exist, in addition to worrying less about money, career, and children.

SKIN HEALTH

I want to share a personal story about my own health journey in the hope it may help somebody. About 3 years ago, I began suffering from a mild skin rash on parts of my body in the typical eczema prone locations such as behind the knees and elbows. I never had any skin issues up to this point, and grew up very active and sporty. My lifestyle did not change around this time; I had been working for the same employer for 4 years and living in the same city and flat. After giving the skin a couple of weeks to subside without success, I decided to schedule a medical appointment who advised it was typical eczema and prescribed me the standard steroid creams and tablets to take on a mild dose for 5-7 days. These tablets worked well and the skin returned to normal for the following 3-4 months. After this time, my skin rash suddenly returned in a more aggressive form all over my body without any clear trigger. I returned to the doctor again who prescribed me the same dose of medication which quickly cleared the symptoms albeit did not explain the root cause. This back and forth of seemingly healthy skin to inflamed rash continued for a further 4-6 months when I finally came to the conclusion something was not right, and perhaps there was a deeper problem beyond what the doctor advised was a perfectly normal case of eczema.

My family had no previous case of reported eczema or allergies, and so I found it quite difficult to believe I was suddenly the first to experience this inflammation without any obvious driver. In addition, I never had any issues with common trigger foods such as gluten and dairy. I arranged an appointment with a dermatologist who examined common allergies and conducted a skin biopsy. The allergies all came back negative while the biopsy stated the obvious; inflammation of the skin! I was then referred to an immunologist and an allergist who both confirmed all was normal after extensive testing. They subsequently referred me to a gastroenterologist who conducted an endoscopy and colonoscopy, both of which looked normal without any sign of inflammation.

At this stage, I was pretty gutted as I was going back and forth without any progress on understanding my situation, and at the same time my skin was getting worse. After 12 months of expensive testing with no results I felt really disheartened, and was convinced there were others with similar distressing, helpless journeys. Over the next 6 months, I persisted to seek answers and scheduled further appointments with various dermatologists to seek a second opinion (the long wait times didn't help my case), and at the same pursued alternative medical paths such as a nutritionist, dietician, psychologist, kinesiologist, herbalist, and a natural healer, most of whom were none the wiser. I also signed up for a full medical check-up at my local hospital in case anything came up potentially relevant to my condition. Thankfully all results came back normal, and the funny thing in hindsight was that almost every doctor I saw suggested a different condition ranging from eczema, dermatitis, rosacea, dermatitis herpetiformis, urticaria, hives, ulcers, acne, scabies, candida, and even ringworms among others!

I was so upset that my mental health began to suffer. I went from working out almost every day and eating a balanced diet with 8% body fat and a metabolic age of 12, to no strenuous exercise at all for fear of exacerbating my skin inflammation. I also lost contact with friends and missed out on many social activities and weddings. To clarify, I am not seeking sympathy and realise my issue was very much a first world problem compared to so many others suffering in silence. However, my main frustration was that nobody was taking this seriously other than myself, and traditional medicine had me running around chasing my tail. My family were quite dismissive at first and put it down to stress management and lifestyle, while the few trusted friends in the loop found it difficult to imagine I was in the state I described!

I couldn't understand why this was happening to me and why now.

After 18 months of searching for answers, I was still at a loss to understand my illness, despite studying the skin online for hours on end most days. I slowly began to realise my issue likely had nothing to do with my skin at all, and this realisation was the start of my turning point. Incredibly, no doctor had raised such a possibility and I learned through my own self-reading it was likely an internal gut problem that needed fixing. While the medical results clearly showed I did not have any food allergies, I learned there is also a medical term called 'food intolerance', and I felt this could be my issue. I decided to undergo a hard-core cleanse and juiced on fruit and vegetables for 30 days in the hope of assisting my healing process. While my skin did gradually clear up and the juice diet definitely helped to remove any toxins and inflammation, I knew this was not a sustainable path as I was losing a lot of body weight and muscle mass during this period.

Next, I decided to remove the most common trigger foods from my diet such as gluten, dairy, and nuts. I focused on plant-based wholefoods for the next 12 months which, while not easy, helped my recovery process a great deal and I got to a place where my skin was clear for 6 months straight. However, I then relapsed again a couple of times over the following months and this was a new low for me. Every relapse has such a damaging psychological impact as you feel like you have made so much progress and then all of a sudden it comes crashing down, as unlike bloating or cramps which can pass within hours, it can take up to 2 weeks for your skin to recover again in my experience. Your career suffers, your relationships suffer, and your confidence suffers big time!

I began to spend an hour every day reading academic papers on subjects ranging from diet, intermittent fasting, histamine response, topical steroid withdrawal, gluten sensitivity, gut health, fungal infections, allergies and genetics among many other topics. I got to the point where I was confident I had narrowed down my own symptoms to a handful of conditions and decided from that point, I would no longer waste my money on doctors and instead take matters into my own hands. To be honest I was very fortunate my girlfriend was a nutritionist, yoga instructor, and super into her own healthy eating and wellbeing. This served as a positive influence on me and I encourage you to have similar positive energy supporting you too.

REGRETS

One of the issues I found with Western doctors is they typically only treat the symptoms. While this can work well with a broken leg, I regret treating my skin rash with prescribed immune suppressing drugs in order to mask my symptoms in the short term. Instead I should have paid closer attention to my biomarkers such as what I was eating, my sleeping patterns, exercise regime, hydration, and daily stress levels among other factors. To be clear, I am not for a moment suggesting poor direction, I am simply sharing my experience, and from speaking with other sufferers, many people have encountered similar guidance.

One of the main mistakes I made along the journey was to focus too much on the symptoms rather than on the root cause. I needed to address the underlying problem which was the kidney, liver, digestion, and overall internal gut health. I was applying all the ointments and creams prescribed by my doctor however it turns out I was focusing on the wrong factors. The root problem was internal namely addressing the digestive system, the lymphatic system, and liver function. The skin was simply the catalyst my body was using to scream for help. The root cause of the issue was internal and that's why it was a waste of time for me to see a dermatologist who simply focused on the skin symptoms, which of course is their job and I am not suggesting otherwise!

Another error on my part was quickly moving from one doctor to another, and from one diet to another. Instead, I should have stuck with one doctor for medical supervision, while at the same time focusing on my diet and lifestyle factors. Instead of trusting in the biomarkers, I was waking up each morning and rushing to examine myself in the mirror, obsessed with every slight change. These biomarkers are your most important measure to monitor your progress and understand how your body is feeling. By biomarkers, I refer to sleep quality, digestive issues such as bloating and gas, stool form, energy levels, sex drive, mental health, and memory fog.

PATIENCE

In my experience, the most important aspect of the recovery is to stick with it and be patient. For those of you who have suffered with skin issues for a long time, don't expect one juice cleanse will normalise your skin within a couple of weeks. Do yourself a favour and don't set deadlines, it will only lead to disappointment. There is no timeline on how long it takes to recover. This healthy diet and lifestyle guide represent your new way of life and part of your identity going forward, if you really want to cure. Too often I was placing ambitious deadlines and unrealistic expectations on my skin recovery and biomarkers. The recovery process will be different for everyone and there is no hard and fast deadline for when you can expect your digestive system and skin to recover. For some fortunate people it will be 3 months, while for others it could be a 2-year journey. The point is that you simply need to take it one day at a time, focus on the daily biomarkers and listen to your body in terms of energy and mindset. Control the controllable and you will clear out the toxins and notice results over time!

GUT HEALTH LINK

I eventually learned through my own research that the majority of skin related health issues such as acne, eczema, psoriasis can all be linked back to the state of our gut health. My anxiety only exacerbated the problem and it is no coincidence those suffering from skin disorders also report higher levels of stress, depression, and digestive problems. I believe this demonstrates how the conventional medicinal approach to specialisation of body parts and organs can sometimes limit our ability to receive adequate care in cases where we have an obvious symptom caused by a relationship between different parts of our body. One obvious sign of the relationship between the skin and the gut is when bloating, gas, and diarrhea start presenting themselves during times of our skin rash flair-ups, emphasising again the importance of listening to our biomarkers.

In fact, many of these inflammatory biomarker signals can point to intestinal permeability or more commonly called leaky gut. Leaky gut is a condition allowing partially digested food particles into the blood system, which then move around the body causing widespread inflammation both internally and often externally in the form of skin disorders. In essence, the skin has no part to play regardless of how inflamed it may appear, which is why I took issue waiting 6 months to see a dermatologist who doesn't even focus on the internal gut issue!

For a healthy person, the gut serves as a gate keeper preventing partially digested foods from entering into the blood system, and only allowing fully digested foods to pass through. Studies show close to 50% of people suffering with skin rashes also complain about digestive issues including constipation, and have a larger amount of 'bad bacteria' in their stool. And the fact is that increasing numbers of people are suffering; according to some reports, only 1 in 10 people in the US complained of allergies and gut related issues in the 1960s, compared with as many as 1 in 3 people today. To make matters worse, the research clearly demonstrates that regular inflammation is linked to various ancillary illnesses including cancer, depression, and chronic anxiety. In my own case, I lost more than 10kg from peak to trough within 2 years and found it difficult to get outside and exercise as my skin rash would get very itchy. In addition, my social life was turned upside down and even outdoor walks were restricted due to my cracked skin. I found it particularly difficult when well-meaning friends and family would suggest a simple solution such as washing detergent, stress, and shampoo as if I wasn't aware of these basic possible triggers! On the positive side, I eventually did get myself sorted through strict diet and eliminating trigger foods through a 3 phase approach which I want to share with you. It took massive resolve as I put all my effort and attention toward my recovery process, digestion, and skin health above all else including relationships, career, and sociability. I relearned how to socialise and play sports again, and when I finally got to a place where I was healthy, I had a new-found appreciation for life!

THE 3 PHASE APPROACH

My recovery program consisted of 3 phases. Phase 1 is all about cleansing and allowing your body to rid itself of the internal toxins. This is without doubt the hardest of the 3 phases and involves the most sacrifice. Each phase is equally important and progressive; one cannot move onto phase 2 until phase 1 is entirely complete and the same applies for moving to phase 3 without first completing phase 2. Phase 1 is focused on drinking water, intermittent fasting, salt flushes, and regular juicing. In other words, detoxifying the body!

PHASE 1 - The first step in phase 1 is to conduct a water fast for 1-3 days depending on how comfortable you feel doing it. For me I started out on a 60-hour program of only drinking water. One simple tip for extending your water fast is to start in the evening after your dinner. This way, you have notched up 12 hours when you wake up the next morning and have some strong momentum behind you. There is no magic formula for how long you should water fast, however from my own reading of nutritional papers, two days seems to be the minimum required time to gain any meaningful results. As a general guide, the heavier you are and the more body weight you have to lose, the longer the water fast duration should be up to a max of 3 days (accompanied by medical supervision of course!). The purpose of the water fast is to remove all the foods in your body, reduce inflammation, and measurably improve your gut microbiome. In addition, there are many ancillary benefits such as lower blood pressure, improved metabolism and cardiovascular health.

After you complete your water fast you then ease into a juice cleansing diet for at least half the time you did your water fast. For example, if you have done a 2-day water fast you then ease back into nourishing your body with a 1-day juice cleanse. This should include drinking a combination of juices and water for each meal throughout the day. Suggested juices for this cleanse include lettuce, cucumber, and celery. After this 1- day juice cleanse you can then introduce a nourishing diet of both juicing and eating a variety of fruits and vegetables. These are your core pillar foods during phase 1, in tandem with a juice fast every other week. In addition, you should also be doing regular salt flushes during phase 1 which I will explain now.

A saltwater flush is simply drinking 300ml to 500ml of water with 2 teaspoons of salt. This will clear out your colon and detoxify your body, and also help to rinse out any build-up of waste and parasites from your digestive tract. About 45 minutes after drinking the salt water, you will need to use the bathroom, so make sure you stay close by after you drink the salt flush! There is lots of information online about the benefits so read about it if you feel unsure. I know I was deeply skeptical about it initially and spent a lot of time researching the subject before committing. The best time of the day to do the saltwater flush is first thing in the morning before consuming any foods. I like to do it during my water fasting on the morning of day 2 as my body is in the process of clearing out foods already and the saltwater flush can accelerate the process. The most important factor is to do the flush on an empty stomach.

Overall phase 1 should go on for about 1-3 months depending on how your body responds. If you have already been eating plant-based wholefood for a number of years, you will likely only need to go through phase 1 for a couple of weeks to a month. However, if you are new to dieting and quite overweight, you should try to commit to phase 1 for 2-3 months based on your body's response signals. The biomarkers are your feedback mechanism, and if you have lots of skin rash flair-ups, low energy levels, poor quality sleep, and regular bloating, then you should consider continuing on phase 1 for longer in order to fully cleanse your body. On the other hand, if your biomarkers feel healthy and your skin is quickly normalising, then you can move onto phase 2 of the process after 2-4 weeks. The key to phase 1 is to focus on your biomarkers and trust in the cleansing process. The more serious you take your skin disease, the sooner your body will build a core foundation for your gut microbiome to advance to phase 2. Make no mistake, your commitment to phase 1 will determine how quickly your skin will fully recover or otherwise!

For phase 1 a good reference point to go by in terms of your diet is the 80/10/10, developed by Dr Douglas Graham who promotes a low-fat raw vegan approach, and has a book by the same name. The diet recommends obtaining at least 80% of your total daily calories from carbohydrates while limiting your fats and protein intake to 10% of total calories. It is really important for your skin recovery to keep a healthy ratio between your carbs to fat of at least 5:1 in order to support your gut and skin health recovery. While many experts will suggest you can load up on nuts, avocados and seeds, this is not the case on this diet as we want to stick with low fat, raw vegan foods, maintaining a high carb to fat ratio. Foods to focus on during the 80/10/10 macro-nutrient diet are fruits (and lots of them), vegetables, and healthy wholefood carbs such as oatmeal and rice varieties. 80/10/10 is shown to improve digestion, boost energy, and most importantly for us, cleanse and improve the gut health. The focus of this diet is to clear out your body and does not necessarily represent a long-term diet alternative. In fact, I personally would not recommend this as a long-term solution given the very high fruit intake specifically.

PHASE 2 – Phase 2 of your healing process sets the stage for your recovery and is focused on identifying the foods that you can eat on a daily basis. The duration of phase 2 will be determined by the number of foods you decide to test through your elimination diet process. Start super simple by choosing a select few plant-based wholefoods that have never given you any trouble in the past, and then expand from there. For example, you could start with brown rice, sweet potato, and lettuce by eating these foods only for 1 week to allow your body detoxify, and to ensure none of these 3 foods are causing you any issues. Listen carefully to your biomarkers and take notes if a food is causing trouble and promptly eliminate it.

On this point, it is really important to keep an elimination diet journal where you can monitor your progress. For the first month, try to keep your food combinations simple. The reason for starting on the plant-based wholefood approach is because we are suffering from an imbalance in our body, and we need to completely detoxify and cleanse our gut microbiome. Think about the vegan diet as hitting the crucial reset button. After month 1, you will have built up a solid information resource of your foundation foods, and then you can start to experiment and branch out into new foods such as meats and nightshade vegetables. Each week add 1 food to allow your body to get used to eating each new food in turn, and continue the process of journaling and tracking your biomarkers. Journaling will enable you to keep tabs on progress, and identify which foods work for you. Write down your daily meals and how your biomarkers feel afterwards. There is no rush in getting through phase 2 so take your time to experiment with food types. The longer you stay in phase 2 the easier your transition into phase 3 will be, and you will know it is time when you feel really comfortable with your diet. The key is to be consistent, and don't get tempted to retry foods that cause you trouble; it is not worth it and your body will be grateful!

PHASE 3 – Phase 3 of the diet is all about consolidation and maintaining your focus on healthy eating. This is the time where you can start to make diet adjustments now that you fully understand what you can eat. Phase 3 is really the beginning of your new self, armed with the valuable tools you have gained over the first two phases. Exercise continues to play a critical role in phase 3, as it is so important for healing your body and internal lymphatic pipeline. Exercising rids your system of toxins and baggage as you move and sweat. While some people will heal quicker than others, focusing on the timeline to recovery is really missing the point and not the way to assess your progress. The solution is simply consistent healthy eating and daily movement whether gym work, cardio, hiking, sports, or swims, and the timeframe is completely irrelevant because either way, time will pass whether you have clear skin or a rash!

Even in phase 3, it is still appropriate to maintain your daily journal and update how you are feeling in terms of your biomarkers. In addition, note any new food varieties and combinations you may be eating. This will then allow you to reflect and piece together potential new trigger foods you were not aware of. During this phase it is more likely that trigger foods will cause digestive issues rather than outright skin rash outbreaks. Given you have already rebuilt your gut lining wall during the heroic efforts of phase 1 and 2, it should take time to trigger another skin flair-up outright, however this will come back if you continue to make the same mistakes with trigger foods. Phase 3 is a long-term process of accumulating your daily habits.

Phase 3 is actually much easier than phase 2 in many ways, as it is simply about maintaining the hard-earned results you achieved during phase 2 in terms of fully understanding your elimination diet. Phase 3 should feel enjoyable and rewarding, as it is all about healthy eating and understanding your body on a consistent basis. It is your opportunity to take full responsibility for yourself and not be concerned with what others are eating. Remember what works for others does not necessarily mean it will work for you! There are many people out there who suffer from banana and watermelon intolerances despite the healthy nature of these foods. Broccoli and kiwi are also common trigger foods for people which is surprising given they are often touted as among the healthiest foods out there!

NOURISHING FOODS

Diet represents 50% of your healing process and refers to both the foods you should be focusing on and equally the foods to avoid. Unfortunately, both must work together as without the two, your recovery will not bear fruit. It is imperative that you are super disciplined on eating the right foods, and at the same time avoiding the problematic foods. While gluten may be a common trigger food for many people, it doesn't necessarily mean you must avoid it. It is up to you to sample foods in a controlled environment as part of your elimination diet. Your body will let you know whether you can eat it or not through your gut and digestive feedback process. That being said, there are a number of foods you should consider as part of your core staple diet in order to give your body the best chance of recovery. These foods are easy to digest wholefoods, with a powerful balance of vitamins, minerals, fiber, and anti-oxidant properties to support your gut health recovery:

1) Fresh fruits such as berries, papaya, apples, and pears. Most of the fresh fruit variety are helpful for your skin recovery albeit I have singled out these four as they hold particularly powerful properties to boost your gut diversity (berries for their anti-oxidant properties, and the apples and pears which are full of vitamins, minerals, and high in fiber).

2) Organic fresh wild salmon, hake, and cod, sustainably sourced for extra health properties.

3) Grass-fed organic meat such as beef, venison, liver, and lamb. Grass-fed is important here and will ensure your gut gains the most nourishing bacteria and nutrient profile from the meat.

4) Green vegetables such as lettuce, celery, cucumber, and cabbage work particularly well in juices. They are rich in antioxidants, anti-inflammatory and detoxification properties, as well as high in nutrients and vitamins. Celery in particular contains lots of minerals and electrolytes which have a cleansing and detoxifying effect on the body.

5) Sauerkraut is a very easy to digest fiber with lots of vitamins particularly important for healing your skin disease.

6) Organic eggs and probiotic natural yoghurt.

7) Turmeric and ginger both have strong anti-inflammatory and detoxification properties for the body.

8) Lemon works wonderfully as a cleansing mechanism for the liver, kidneys, and lymphatic system.

On the flip side, there are a number of key foods to avoid in order to resolve your skin issue and restore your gut health. As we discussed, the skin is the signal your body uses to scream out for help, and alert you to the fact there is an internal problem to address. It took me a lot of research and flair-ups to understand which trigger foods were causing my issues and that's what I want to share now:

1) Coffee – Despite what many people say about coffee being healthy, for those of you suffering from skin related problems whether dermatitis, eczema, psoriasis, leaky gut, among others, coffee is making your situation worse. Coffee is very acidic and far too stimulating for the digestive and immune systems. In order to cure the skin, we are trying to calm our skin down to a relaxed and cleansing state, and coffee works in the opposite way as its acidity creates lasting problems in our gut microbiome.

2) Dairy – All forms of dairy should be avoided in order to cure the skin. Dairy has no antioxidant or fiber properties and both are critical to curing your skin condition and overall gut health. In addition, it doesn't host the necessary water properties or vitamins required to fully cure.

3) Processed foods – This is quite a broad bucket and so let me simplify; anything not wholefood based will not be healthy for our gut health and this unfortunately includes all fast food!

4) Gluten – Can be difficult to digest and promotes inflammation and gut issues in people, which can manifest itself into skin problems too.

5) Nuts – There is a reason why so many people report a fatal allergy to nuts. Nuts are difficult to digest and the fat content is very high.

6) Spicy foods – Spices can cause issues for people with skin problems as they are difficult to digest and can delay your healing process. It is fine to have moderate spicy foods occasionally, but you don't want to be eating chunks of pepper, chili flakes, or strong curry paste.

GUT MICROBIOME

The gut microbiome holds the key to your recovery. While research into the gut is at a relatively early stage, studies by various academics suggest the gut microbiome can impact everything from your mood and overall happiness to the quality of your immune system, stress levels, brain health, and of course your skin health. The microbiome is a vast ecosystem of organisms including fungi, yeast, and bacteria. These bacteria are key to our ability to digest and break down our food. It is when our gut microbiome is overcrowded with bad bacteria, that we can suffer digestive issues and skin disease. This is why many of us choose to take probiotic supplements to improve the healthy bacteria ratio in our gut and boost our overall healthy gut flora. It is no wonder the probiotics market is expected to double in value globally between 2015 and 2023 according to some estimates. While it is important to note that supplements can't solely replace a healthy diet, they can certainly help the cause. A healthy gut translates into a healthy immune system and vice versa, and it is this healthy immune system which fights off bacteria, fungus, yeast, and infections from harming the body in times of stress. In addition, it is a healthy immune system that avoids overreacting when certain foods such as gluten, dairy, and nuts enter our body.

Thankfully, research suggests the gut microbiome can be improved through many factors both nutrition and lifestyle related, and these tools can drastically improve our nervous system inflammatory response. The microbiome is partially driven by our genetics and our environmental factors such as stress, gender, demographics, diet, and even athletic ability! In terms of nutrition, taking a well-balanced probiotic supplement, eating a healthy diet full of fruits and vegetables, along with regular intermittent fasting can greatly improve gut flora and boost overall wellbeing. Some people will recommend supplements such as vitamins and fish oils, however there are many studies out there which suggest people don't notice a difference between these supplements when compared with a placebo, so choose wisely and do the research first! In addition, lifestyle factors such as Epsom salt bathing, exercise, exposure to nature and sunlight can all indirectly help your gut flora!

It is worth noting that many of the nutritionists, herbalists, and alternative medical professionals often take a cut of any supplement sales they recommend. In fact, some will have an arrangement with the supplier to purchase the supplements at a 20 to 30% discount, before selling the product to you at market prices, thereby pocketing the difference. While I am not suggesting this happens on a regular basis, I do think it is important to ask upfront for transparency on pricing and any potential conflict of interest in marketing health supplements. To my understanding, there is no such thing as a medication that does not have a side-effect (apart from sleep as we discussed earlier!), so ensure you are in control of the situation and fully understand the fine print first!

FOOD COMBINATIONS

There are so many diet fads out there, one can be forgiven for feeling confused about what to follow:

'Drink lemon water as soon as you wake up'

'Don't drink any water during meals'

'Coffee should not be consumed after a meal as it flushes away the nutrients'

'Only eat fruit after a meal and not beforehand'

This last one I find particularly confusing given we often see menu choices with fruit as a starter and a dessert! As if it couldn't get any more complicated, then you add in the concept of 'food combination'. Food combining makes sense in theory, given that different foods digest at various rates in the body and so should be eaten at particular times. Therefore, certain foods should be eaten together in order to complement and create the optimal digestive process. We have all heard of the food pyramid to explain the nutritional content of foods. Well, there is also a food pyramid for food combinations which you will easily find online. In summary, it suggests that combining proteins and starches should be avoided in the same meal, despite the fact most of us have been brought up enjoying staples such as bangers and mash, fish and chips, and of course spaghetti bolognaise!

The logic is that carbohydrates require an alkaline environment to digest, while protein needs an acidic environment. In addition, the studies suggest that fruits should only be enjoyed on an empty stomach to achieve optimal digestion and certainly not after a meal as dessert! Also, fruit and vegetables should not be consumed at the same time as they have different biochemical properties, according to the research. The overarching concept is we have different enzymes in our body to digest proteins and carbohydrates, and combining both food types at the same time creates digestive issues and an overburdened gut. As a result, certain foods which do not immediately digest properly are left to ferment in your system, causing gas, bloating, and constipation in many cases. The benefits of food combining include less bloating and gas, more energy and weight loss, improved absorption of nutrients, and as a result better overall digestion and skin clarity. However, as with everything, it is up to you to decide for yourself whether it is worth the hassle to follow in practice!

STRESS

The relationship between your skin and overall body health with stress is very strong. As we have already discussed, stress levels have been increasing dramatically as we work longer hours, put more demands on our body, and eat more refined foods. While moderate levels of stress are healthy, sustained chronic stress causes our body problems both physically and mentally. Chronic stress can actually alter our gut function by reducing the production of stomach acid which is critical for our proper food digestion. Unfortunately, it can also negatively impact our hormones, often leading to emotional issues, an overproduction of cortisol and bad bacteria. The amazing part of my recovery was as soon as I stopped obsessing about my skin and rushing to the mirror first thing every morning, the quicker my recovery. Constantly monitoring your skin and worrying about your latest relapse causes emotional stress which worsens the condition further as we have seen. Instead, I invite you to focus your positive energy on the following recovery tools which are firmly under your control:

Diet – we can reduce the physical stress we add to our body by managing our diet and eating healthy wholefoods as we have described in detail. Minimise processed foods and focus on your biomarkers in terms of avoiding foods which cause you bloating, allergies, and inflammation. Remember what works for one person may not work for you. Try to limit your alcohol, caffeine, unnecessary medication, and smoking as these are stressors on the body.

Exercise – make time for at least 30 minutes of exercise per day. Move the body and lymphatic system by walking, stretching, swimming, and cycling among many other forms of exercise. Some studies suggest excessive sitting is worse for our health than smoking so try to get up regularly and move about. Exercise also has huge psychological benefits and helps our brain's cognitive function in terms of numerical and reading ability across all ages. Studies by Professor Babyak on a group of clinically depressed people showed just 3 days per week of exercise for 30 minutes had a greater impact on wellbeing, than taking prescribed anti-depressant medication. After a 16-week period, about half of the prescribed medication group recovered from their condition while an incredible 90% of people in the exercise cohort made a full recovery! Think about that!

Sleep – consistent sleep is crucial for our gut health and reducing inflammation in the body. An erratic sleep routine can lead to increased risk of depression, anxiety, and diabetes among other problems.

Have fun – laughing and having fun is one of the best ways to reduce stress levels. I have a wonderful Aunt who reminds me of this all the time! Meet up with friends, express your creativity, and watch comedy shows to enjoy yourself. Surround yourself with good people who bring out the best in you, and help you to feel good about yourself. Avoid those who drag you down as this impacts your wellbeing and gut microbiome – life is too short! The people you spend time with will affect your mood, mindset, and energy levels, so maintain strong relationships with people whose company you enjoy in order to aid your healing process and gut health in a major way!

Meditation – create awareness in the moment for 10 to 15 minutes per day as it can literally add years onto your life, and have a really positive impact on your emotional, physical, and gut health according to the experts. My preferred technique as an amateur is to concentrate on my breathing to the count of 100. Every time my mind wanders, I try to bring my attention back to each breath. Reading is another great way to focus in the moment, to relax, and rid your mind of constant distraction. According to one recent study, the average person has over 6,000 thoughts per day so that is a lot of distraction to overcome!

LIFESTYLE CHOICES

In order to fully recover you really need to do everything in your control to manage your lifestyle, not only in terms of diet, but also in terms of regular exercise and stimulation. Your body needs to be actively moving around to work your joints, and to aid your digestion and immune system. We all know regular exercise is healthy as part of a balanced lifestyle and these health benefits are also relevant to your skin health and digestion. Taking a regular walk in nature, getting to the gym, playing sports, learning how to cope with stressful situations (breathing techniques, reading, and mindfulness), and getting cold water exposure through ice baths and cold showers are all very healthy for your skin and will aid your recovery process. In addition, regular cleansing and detoxifying your body in terms of water fasting, intermittent fasting, and salt flushes will also help your recovery. While you can't necessarily speed up your body's healing process a great deal, you can stack the odds in your favour by following these regular activities long after your finish the 3 phases.

For those of you who have been trying to recover for a long time and are not seeing the results, the majority of the time this is because you are not fully focused on your diet. For me, diet was by far the most difficult aspect of my recovery process. Adjusting from eating lean meats, mixed nuts and a full Irish breakfast with coffee, to following a super strict and exclusively plant-based wholefood diet takes huge mental discipline. However, the key to overcoming your skin disease and thriving is to think about the alternative of aggravated skin for the rest of your days. It is crucial to put the necessary time and resources into preparing your body and mindset, there is no opportunity cost here. The positive news is your recovery is 100% in your control and you can fully train your mind to work with you on this!

MENTAL HEALTH

Psychology is also so important as part of your recovery. The reality is your mental strength will fluctuate throughout the process of healing. It is not easy to suffer another full-blown skin flair-up after 6 months of clear skin. This really puts your mental resilience to the test and stretches your ability to stay focused on your end goal. Remember it is a marathon and not a sprint, and everybody suffers relapses throughout the process. Sometimes it can be due to a trigger food but often it's a sign of your body detoxifying further and actually making great progress toward fully healing. Don't be disheartened by it and make sure you have a support network to get behind you.

Keep up the consistency, stay persistent, and be positive! It is important not to worry about these relapses, as anxiety and stress are clinically shown to worsen skin related symptoms. Be patient with yourself; there is no end goal here, once your skin is clear it becomes a lifestyle choice to keep it that way so take your time on the journey and trust in the process. Don't be distracted by what your skin looks like on a day to day basis; focus on your biomarkers and not on the surface of your skin. Remember this is not a skin issue, this is a gut and digestion deficiency. While your skin can mess with you, your biomarkers speak the truth so pay close attention to them!

QUOTES ON HEALTH

'Early to bed and early to rise, makes a man healthy, wealthy, and wise' – Benjamin Franklin

'The health you enjoy is largely your choice' – Abraham Lincoln

'For myself I am an optimist - it does not seem to be much use being anything else' – Winston Churchill

'Illness of any kind is hardly a thing to be encouraged in others. Health is the primary duty of life' – Oscar Wilde

'A pessimist sees the difficulty in every opportunity; an optimist sees the opportunity in every difficulty' – Winston Churchill

PART VI

WELLBEING

NUDGING YOUR HAPPINESS

We all want to live well and be happy. However, it is becoming increasingly difficult to achieve consistent happiness because of the way society pressures us to behave. Happiness indicators have been steadily falling across most countries, and I want to share a number of trusted techniques backed by scientific research which can help you become happier! As you know, happiness can have so many positive derivative side effects in our life. For example, a 2007 study of roughly 7,000 adults showed those who described themselves as happy were more likely to eat fresh fruit and vegetables and regularly exercise compared to others. Happiness also impacts our sleep quality, stress management, weight, and wider quality friendships. Despite all of these very tangible benefits, many of us put little thought or effort into the practice of happiness yet actively spend 2 minutes twice a day brushing our teeth!

In reality everything you think will make you happy probably won't! Most of us believe landing the dream job, earning the big pay-check, winning the lottery, and buying the nice car will make us much happier but the reality is quite different. For example, a famous study by Brickman and colleagues studied lottery winners one year on from their success, compared with a control group who did not have success, and found their overall happiness was almost identical. It turns out the initial honeymoon period of winning the lottery quickly fades, and we set a new reference point which normalises our happiness levels again over a remarkably short period of time.

On missing out on the dream job, research clearly demonstrates no material impact on our overall happiness. A famous study done by psychologist Dan Gilbert neatly showed college students who were turned down from their dream job demonstrated only a marginal decline in their wellbeing. When the rejection decision was deemed fair by the student, the decline in happiness was much less than 1 out of 10 and when the decision was deemed unfair, there was no decline in reported happiness at all. Other common beliefs are weight loss and cosmetics can make us happier than we think. However specific research projects have demonstrated achieving weight loss and carrying out cosmetics of any kind has no positive impact on our happiness scores, and in fact is more likely to negatively impact our long-term happiness!

So, what does impact happiness if not the above items. Well it turns out genetics does play a significant role. Some people really do see the world from a more positive standpoint, and it is estimated that genetics can determine up to 50% of our happiness disposition. Life circumstances such as winning the lottery, our purpose, and keeping healthy, contribute only 10%, while the controllables such as actions, habits, intentions, and relationships make up the remaining 40%. This is actually really positive news in my view, as it shows a minimum of 40% of our outlook on life and overall satisfaction is very much under our control. Acts such as showing kindness to another person is a great way to improve your own wellbeing as we have touched on already. Donating blood, phoning a friend, giving to charity, and cooking a meal for a loved one are all very tangible ways of boosting your wellbeing score.

MORE MONEY, LESS HAPPY

Contrary to what most of us believe, money does not make us happier beyond a certain point. Studies show the threshold is a salary of $75,000 per year in the US and £50,000 in the UK, with any additional income having no impact on our overall wellbeing. These levels were calculated by Professors Daniel Kahneman and Angus Deaton of Princeton University, and their landmark study of almost 500,000 Americans showed 'emotional wellbeing' plateaus for those earning more than $75,000 per year. By emotional wellbeing, they incorporated levels of reported stress, daily positivity in terms of visual smiling and satisfaction, and a lack of worry or sadness. The measure was calculated by asking participants questions such as, 1) How happy are you today? 2) How stressed do you feel? 3) How worried or sad do you feel? Overall the study showed that while people who earn more money think their life should be better as a result, the reality is quite different in that money does not improve our happiness above this $75,000 threshold. In others words, once our basic needs such as healthcare, clean water, and education are met, our happiness stagnates.

Another interesting perspective to assess is the level of reported happiness today compared with history. While average income, equity markets, house prices, longevity, and overall health measures have increased significantly over the past 50 years, reported happiness levels taken across countries have actually declined or stayed constant. In other words, despite the average person enjoying more wealth creation and a wider range of household facilities such as reliable heating and hot water, overall wellbeing has not improved co-measurably, and in many cases has actually fallen. If this is not a wake-up call that we are doing something wrong as a society, I don't know what is!

Breaking this down further, a recent City and Guilds survey showed almost 90% of florists were happy in their work compared with just over 60% of lawyers. While it is possible florists have a natural disposition to be happy, and lawyers are in the job due to the social prestige, when you think about it, florists are working everyday with nature, meeting people who want to go to their store, see the direct results of their work on a daily basis, have great control and creativity in their craft, and generally practice more autonomy compared with the corporate gig. However, our mind suggests lawyers should be happier because their work is deemed high paying and more prestigious. Similarly, another study by the Legatum Institute showed the highest paid roles such as CEO and President did not have the highest life satisfaction. In fact, in many cases it was the staff working as secretary or analyst who displayed the highest scores despite their generally lower pay. In a similar vein, too many of us often describe our jobs as really dull, complain about our colleagues and work place culture, crave more autonomy and respect from our manager, and yet convince ourselves we are really happy and want to make partner! On the other end of the spectrum, it is the farmers, priests, and fitness instructors who regularly show the highest life satisfaction overall.

It appears one of the main reasons why money doesn't necessarily improve our wellbeing, is because people who earn more also spend more toward upkeeping their lifestyle. In addition, many have to work longer hours and spend more time commuting, both of which detract important leisure time away from family, friends, and hobbies. Society has a habit of valuing people who work longer hours and attain more success, despite the obvious sacrifices involved. Coming back to the study, those working between 21 and 30 hours per week reported the highest wellbeing, while any additional hours beyond this point only detracted from average reported happiness. If this isn't convincing enough, research has shown the worst time of day for the average employee is when they are with their boss, and that people would rather do almost anything else possible other than their work!

SPEND ON OTHER PEOPLE

While earning more money may not improve happiness as we have seen, it turns out spending on others can do! An interesting Canadian study by Professor Dunn showed spending money on other people may have a more positive impact on happiness than spending money on ourselves. The experiment gave individuals either $5 or $20 and asked them to spend the money on themselves or on other people. The results clearly demonstrated those who spent the money on other people reported greater levels of happiness, and the amount of money spent made no difference, despite our intuition the $20 would make us happier than the $5!

EXPERIENCE HAPPY

The science shows that pleasurable experiences make us happier when compared with material possessions. Spending money on a sports game, theatre show, holiday, or restaurant adds more to our happiness than buying those new designer shoes or the latest iPhone! In fact, studies by psychologist Leaf Van Boven at the University of Colorado assess this exact happiness play-off, by asking a large group of people to provide feedback on a purchase they made for $100, where half the group spent the money on an experience and half on a material possession. Specifically, the study asked questions such as how happy does your purchase make you feel, was it good value for money, and how much has it impacted your wellbeing. They found clear results showing those who spent the money on an experience scored higher on happiness, satisfaction, and fulfillment metrics. Interestingly, this theory holds across all income levels and does not discriminate by status or profession – we all win! One unexpected side benefit of an upcoming pleasurable experience is that the anticipation of the experience alone can lead to an increase in our happiness! However, people don't believe this to be the case as demonstrated with a now famous study by psychologist Howell from San Francisco State University, who demonstrated that while we believe in advance of a purchase that the possession will give us double the happiness of an experience, the results showed this is not the case and that our mind is playing games with us as we already know it likes to do!

Other benefits of an experience over a material possession include the fact that experiences tend to be healthier and more active. Many of our favourite experiences invite us to explore nature and the outdoors, often involve interacting with other people, and actually make others like us more in the process according to the research! Nobody likes to hear people boasting about their new expensive iPad as it can make others feel jealous, so it makes sense people prefer to hear about our latest adventures, as it can often spur others to do the same!

MATERIAL HAPPINESS

We now know experiences trump material possessions; however, the question is often asked about the impact of material possessions on our happiness. An interesting study by psychologist Raymond Nickerson in 2003 showed craving material items such as the latest iPad or a new pair of shoes can have a strong negative impact on our overall reported life satisfaction. He measured the materialistic attitudes of over 10,000 freshmen in the 1970s, and then came back to the same participants 20 years later to find out how their life was stacking up. He found clear data to show non-materialistic people reported significantly higher life satisfaction compared with those who placed a premium on material possessions. It was also found that the materialistic cohort showed greater mental health issues compared with the non-materialistic group. I think this is particularly apt in today's society where we are so pressured into keeping up with others and having the latest fashion accessories.

TREAT OTHERS NICELY

It turns out being kind to others can boost your own happiness too. A favourite study from Professor Otake and colleagues in Japan showed happy people become happier through acts of kindness toward others. To demonstrate, the researchers divided a sample group into those who reported feeling happy and unhappy. They subsequently tested both group's motivation to conduct acts of kindness on others, their memory of recent kindness shown upon them, and subsequent positive behaviours. The results showed the happier group demonstrated significantly higher scores on all three factors compared with the unhappy group. The study then asked both groups to reflect on recent acts of kindness and to write them down, with the results showing that those able to recall recent acts of kindness demonstrated materially higher levels of happiness. Interestingly, other research has shown that increasing our outright number of kindly acts per day can measurably improve our happiness which dovetails nicely with the Japanese study findings too!

SOCIAL CONNECTION

Our feeling of social inclusion is another big driver of positive wellbeing, and can boost our physical health, and even make us more likely to recover from an illness according to the science. People who report feeling happy, spend more quality time with friends and family, and have stronger friendships, family ties, and romantic relationships compared to others. Psychologist Boothby, from the University of Pennsylvania, studied this phenomenon of social impact and demonstrated how shared experiences are amplified. She conducted a simple experiment asking individuals to eat a chocolate bar in pairs. Participants reported enjoying the chocolate more when they ate it with another person compared to eating it alone, despite not knowing or communicating with the other person during the said experience. Simply knowing this outcome can have many wide-ranging implications in our daily lives from going to the cinema with friends, playing sports with others, and even finding a romantic partner whom you can share experiences together! Arguably, this goes to the very core of why married couples report higher levels of happiness compared with singletons. Perhaps the same rules could be applied to our daily commute to work, where we could easily add to our happiness by striking up a conversation with the stranger sitting next to us!

EXERCISE

Exercise is another critical part of living a full and happy life, and can include going out for a walk, spending time gardening, or even playing golf. The focus should be on getting the heart rate up, stretching the legs, clearing the mind, and breathing in some fresh air. This should ideally be done on a daily basis where possible and can be implemented into your morning commute to work, stepping out to grab a lunchtime sandwich, or getting to the gym or on the bike in the evening. Recently, the trend is interactive classes such as HIIT, pilates, dance, and yoga which are taking over the local parks, and tends to foster that extra sense of motivation and achievement which comes with working out in groups!

As a side note, if you are looking to increase your chances on the first date then read on! Believe it or not, behavioural economists have shown that getting your heart rate elevated can improve your sexual attraction. Perhaps this explains the explosive popularity of the group exercise classes! Based on the research, going for a light run or cycle together on a first date will improve your sexual attraction to each other! Other benefits of exercise include reporting more energy, happiness, focus, longevity, and work ethic. In addition, exercise has also been shown to significantly reduce stress, without any side effects. Imagine if these outcomes could be captured in a medical drug, it would surely be the most valuable pharmaceutical product ever made! For me, one of the best things about exercise is that even if I am having a bad day in work or with family matters, getting out for some exercise almost instantly helps me feel better and more energised.

GRATITUDE

Arguably the most significant tool to improve your happiness is by practicing gratitude. Gratitude is the act of being appreciative of activities and relationships in life. One such famous study, by Professor Emmons of UCD, asked a third of participants to write down daily up to 5 items they are grateful for, a third to write down 5 daily inconveniences, and the final third to simply write down 5 daily events. All participants were then asked to answer the following 4 questions; 1) how is your life going, 2) how will the upcoming week go for you, 3) how are you feeling physically, and 4) how much exercise did you get today. The results showed that those who practiced the daily gratitude exercises scored materially higher in each of the questions, and showed a significant increase in their overall wellbeing. Equally, writing thank you notes and gratitude letters can improve your wellbeing both immediately after putting pen to paper, and even up to a couple of months after the event. In addition, gratitude can significantly improve personal and professional relationships, both in marriage and in the workplace based on the research. In fact, showing gratitude in the workplace can increase the efficiency of employees, particularly when practiced by senior management. Incredible how the simple act of saying thank you can have such a profound impact in all aspects of society!

MIND GAMES

As we have seen, our mind often plays games by tricking us into believing a certain short-term temptation or satisfaction will have a positive impact. Our mind leads us to believe getting the promotion at work, perfecting your beach body, or finding true love will enhance our happiness, however we have seen from the science this is not the case.

When participating in an activity or hobby such as music, sports, or social activities, there are ways we can effectively trick our mind to enhance our enjoyment of the activity. One study by psychologist Jose demonstrated that sharing hobbies with others, talking about the activity to others, showing signs of physical positive energy, and even thinking about telling others are all scientifically supported methods to enhance your own overall wellbeing! On the contrary, telling yourself you didn't want to sign up for this, thinking about the activity finally ending, and ways it could be improved are sure ways to detract from your experience and weigh down your life satisfaction in the short term!

Another mental tool to boost your happiness is to reignite your memory bank of past positive experiences. A study by Professor Lyubomirsky demonstrated with a sample group, that those who reflected regularly on happy moments reported higher levels of wellbeing when compared to the default group. Thinking about your engagement holiday, ski trip with friends, and memorable family moments are an easy way to boost your mood and overall life satisfaction on a regular basis. In fact, not only did this exercise boost happiness immediately afterwards, but it also showed clear signs of higher wellbeing for as long as one month after the initial exercise!

REFERENCE POINTS

As we can see, the mind works in mysterious ways and reference points are another mental trick impacting our wellbeing. Professor Medvec's famous 'when less is more' study showed that even elite Olympic medal winners experienced very different reference points and happiness on the podium. Through their analysis of video presentations, they found that bronze medal winners showed materially higher happiness levels compared with silver medalists. This makes some sense given the bronze medal winner is probably (on average) fortunate to be on the podium in the first place, and only one spot away from 4th place. However, the silver medal winner may feel hard done by, missing out on the top spot of gold. Unsurprisingly, the study found gold medal winners were the happiest!

These reference points are evident in our daily lives too. We measure our success compared to friends and colleagues in our social circle. We measure our job seniority based on relative salary and job title. In fact, the job title reference point is well known in Silicon Valley where companies often attach a higher sounding job title to a position as a benefit, instead of incremental salary rise in order to attract prospective candidates! This reference point is the very reason why humans are never satisfied. Often, you hear about a billionaire who doesn't want to retire and keeps placing big bets in the market because their reference point of success is constantly shifting depending on how their peers are performing. An interesting study by academics Clark & Oswald demonstrated this point nicely when they studied the job satisfaction of 5,000 workers in the UK whose salary increased, but by comparatively less than their colleagues. The study found that the subjects' average job satisfaction and overall wellbeing actually declined, because others received higher comparative pay increases! In fact, another study was carried out which showed people would prefer to be earning $50,000 when others in their firm were earning $30,000, rather than earning $100,000 when others were earning $150,000 for example. The point being we would rather the lower salary in order to be the highest paid in the room!

Another negative outcome of a reference point relates to our interaction with social media and television. A famous study by Professor Schrum found that the more hours we spend watching television, the less well-off we estimate we are compared to others, and the worse impact it has on our own self-esteem. At the same time, the more television we watch, the more money we spend on material possessions. It is no wonder that anti-depressant medication is now prescribed close to 500 times more often when compared with just 20 years ago, while recent graduates regularly report feeling more unhappy than previous generations. At the same time, body shaming is another big driver of unhappiness and self-esteem issues for people, which is often directly related to social media and advertising posters. A study by Professor Kenrick of ASU showed that looking at pictures of billboard models can significantly impact self-esteem and mood. He rated the happiness of a group of women both before and after seeing the models, and the results clearly demonstrated that the mood of the group was significantly lower after seeing the models. In a similar study, the same academics studied married couples and asked the men to rate the attractiveness of their wife both before and after looking at a picture of models in a magazine. The results were similar and underpin how social comparison can be so dangerous in society!

The good news is we can alter our reference point in order to help improve our happiness. One famous study by

Professor Morewedge (2010) demonstrated the simple act of changing a reference point can impact your overall enjoyment of a certain activity. He invited a group to enjoy eating a packet of tasty crisps. He had one group enjoy the crisps while standing beside a packet of sardines, while another group enjoyed the crisps while standing beside some delicious looking chocolate. The study found that the group standing beside the sardines reported significantly higher enjoyment from eating the crisps, compared with the group standing beside the chocolate!

Another measure to change our reference point is to reflect on when the event first happened. For example, when you were first picked on the sports team, think about how you felt at the time and how proud you were to be on the team. One year later, you may feel like changing teams because you are recently losing games and dressing room morale is not good. However, the research suggests reflecting on how you felt when you first joined can have positive results on your frame of reference. The same can be said with your work situation when things start to go downhill and you contemplate applying for a new job. Try to reflect on how happy you were when you first landed the job offer and joined the team. Also, if you have experienced unemployment or lots of rejections in the past, reflect on how good your current position really is compared to how you felt previously without a job. There is so much to be grateful for in life and often, we simply need to practice reframing our reference point to fully appreciate our current situation.

MINDFUL

Many people argue that happiness is not a feeling but a practice, and that mindfulness is one of the best tools to impact your wellbeing in a positive and consistent way. Science has shown that focusing on the present moment has been used to overcome anxiety and stress for thousands of years by reducing mental clutter and noise, improving self-awareness and circulation, and bolstering attention, focus, and ultimately wellbeing. At the same time, mindfulness can enhance our feeling of social proximity, love, and kindness towards each other, and even increase our probability of saying nice things about others! Another great benefit of mindfulness is that when done correctly our mind is focused on the present moment. The significance of this is that a mind-wandering state can often impact our happiness in a negative way. The reality is that we as humans mind-wander about 50% of our waking hours! Even when we are busy completing a task or working on a project, we are still mind-wandering about 30% of the time according to studies! Believe it or not, the one state when we are not mind wandering is during sexual intercourse – no wonder it makes us feel so happy!

MARRIAGE

Marriage has traditionally been seen as a natural step in life and as a result, the majority of us still treat marriage as a lifetime objective, to such an extent that older people who have yet to marry are often stigmatised as 'unlucky' or yet to meet 'the right one', despite the fact it may be out of choice for them to remain single! In fact, the single life is more popular today than ever before, perhaps at least driven by the shocking statistic that almost 50% of marriages typically end in divorce (precise number depending on the country!). While most of us never expect to be included in this statistic and believe marriage will solve all our problems and result in living 'happily ever after', this is simply not the case. Too often when a relationship ends, we hear a relative or friend remark 'such a shame' or 'they seemed so good together', however rarely do people step back and suggest perhaps it was in their best interest to go their separate ways, and that it will all work out in the end! For those of us who do get married, the average age has moved from our teens well into our early 30s according to national statistics in many countries.

While finding your true love can have a positive impact on wellbeing, it is only for a short period, according to studies by Professor Richard Lucas from Michigan State University. He assessed close to 25,000 people over 15 years and found married people reported higher levels of happiness, but this only lasted for the first 1-2-year honeymoon phase of the marriage. After this time, happiness normalised back to the same level as the singletons. Of course, those who were in unhappy marriages during this time reported significantly lower levels of life satisfaction compared with the default single group. Equally, we cannot forget that divorce generally leads to concerns about the welfare of children from the relationship, and how they may cope with the changes. While studies do show children suffer from anxiety and pain in the short term, they also report improved happiness and relief over the medium and long term after their parents split. Therefore, we can imply it is better to be the children of parents who have divorced and moved on with their lives, rather than children whose parents reluctantly stay together within a toxic environment! Perhaps we should start congratulating people when they divorce as opposed to offering our condolences! A good starting point to improve our societal stigma associated with marriage and divorce would be to set expectations for the next generation. Too many classic books end with the narrative 'they fell in love, got married, and lived happily ever after…' However, we now know that this is not necessarily the case, and marriage can cause immense pain, suffering, and regret when not given the serious consideration it deserves. In my opinion, it is the single most important and impactful career and life decision we can make, and it's about time we start facing up to its challenges!

One piece of research from the acclaimed marriage therapist Dr. John Gottman focused on 130 recently married couples and attempted to predict the likely divorce rate among each of the couples. His research showed the main predictor of divorce was a behavioural pattern of 'contempt', which refers to an underlying tone of criticism, negativity, or sarcasm. One such indication of a successful relationship according to his research is the ratio of positive to negative comments in a given day between couples. For example, complementing your better half's new shoes or figure in a pair of jeans would be considered a positive remark, while sarcastically noting that the freshly prepared coffee is cold would be a negative comment! He advises the sum of such comments should be a minimum ratio of 5:1 every day in order to predict a successful relationship over time. Other tips he recommends for couples include saying good morning and good night to each other daily, committing to a weekly date night, having a low stress conversation when you reunite at the end of every day, displaying affection toward each other such as hugging, kissing, holding each other tenderly, and giving genuine daily appreciation. He finds couples who stick to these small steps spend an average of 5 hours more together each week, and find that their respective relationship and marital happiness increase over time!

FAKE SMILE

The more we smile the happier we become. While I don't think this will come as a surprise to most, the unexpected part is that even forcing ourselves to smile can make us feel happier. One controversial study by Professor Strack asked volunteers to watch cartoons while in one of 3 groups; the first group held a pen between their lips without touching their teeth (stimulates frowning), the second held a pen between their teeth without touching their lips (stimulates smiling), while the third group simply held the pen in their hand. Interestingly, the group with the pen between their teeth found the cartoons the funniest. The simple act of contracting the same muscles used to exercise laughter actually made the subjects happier! However, the science shows that roughly 80% of laughter is used in social situations not because something is funny, but because we are trying to make others like us, diffuse tension, or demonstrate we are not a threat. In addition, the science demonstrates that we are up to 30 times more likely to laugh when we are in the company of others, and that laughter is physically contagious! Yet another reason to spend more quality time with friends!

FINAL WORD

As you can see, wellbeing is incredibly subjective and there is no sudden cure or easy way to find it, other than to know it does not come as we intuitively believe! Our mind is fixated on the dream job, the high salary, and good grades! But in fact, as we have discussed, none of these factors have any meaningful impact on our sustained happiness over the long term. Wellbeing is primarily the sum of our purpose and social interactions. Spending time with people we enjoy and doing work we find engaging and purposeful is far more important than spending time with celebrities, buying the latest gadget, or working in that high-powered job!

QUOTES ON WELLBEING

'Whoever is happy will make others happy too... how wonderful it is that nobody needs wait a single moment before starting to improve the world' – Anne Frank

'Happiness is not in the mere possession of money; it lies in the joy of achievement, in the thrill of creative effort' – Franklin Roosevelt

'Far and away the best prize that life offers is the chance to work hard at work worth doing' – Theodore Roosevelt

'The only way to do great work is to love what you do' – Steve Jobs

'The two most important days in your life are the day you are born and the day you find out why' – Mark Twain

PART VII

PURPOSE

THE MEXICAN FISHERMAN PARABLE

I want to share with you my favourite parable which is about a Mexican fisherman and a banker. You may have heard it before but it packs an important message about finding balance between work and play in my view. It is a topic many of us struggle to optimise in our fast paced, cut-throat society.

The story is about an American investment banker on vacation in a small coastal Mexican village where he meets a fisherman who is busy docking his small fishing boat with several large, freshly caught fish on board. The banker is very impressed with the size of the fish and curiously approaches the fisherman to ask about his latest expedition, and to enquire how long it must have taken to catch such quality fish!

The Mexican replied, "Only a little while." The banker then asked why he didn't stay out longer and catch more fish? The Mexican fisherman replied he had enough to support his family's immediate needs. The American then asked "But what do you do with the rest of your time?"

The Mexican fisherman replied, "I sleep late, fish a little, play with my children, take siesta with my wife, stroll into the village each evening where I sip wine and play guitar with my amigos: I have a full and busy life, señor."

The investment banker scoffed, "I am an Ivy League MBA, and I could help you. You could spend more time fishing and with the proceeds buy a bigger boat, and with the proceeds from the bigger boat you could buy several boats until eventually you would have a whole fleet of fishing boats. Instead of selling your catch to the middleman you could sell directly to the processor, eventually opening your own cannery. You could control the product, processing and distribution."

Then he added, "Of course, you would need to leave this small coastal fishing village and move to Mexico City where you would run your growing enterprise". The Mexican fisherman asked, "But señor, how long will this all take?" To which the American replied, "15-20 years." "But what then?" asked the Mexican.

The American laughed and said, "That's the best part. When the time is right you would announce an IPO and sell your company stock to the public and become very rich. You could make millions". "Millions, señor? Then what?" To which the investment banker replied, "Then you would retire. You could move to a small coastal fishing village where you would sleep late, fish a little, play with your kids, take siesta with your wife, stroll to the village in the evenings where you could sip wine and play your guitar with your amigos."

Of course, this is what this fisherman is already doing with his time and is exactly the point of the story! We can all dream big and hope to retire with lots of money, however it is the simple things money can't buy which we most enjoy. Moving our focus away from material possessions and the latest gadgets is a sure way to reduce stress and anxiety as we have already discussed. Rather than dreaming about the latest iPhone or wide screen television, we can instead imagine ourselves swimming in the fresh salt water and enjoying a beautiful sunset. The most common question asked after reading this parable is which character would you choose to be, the fisherman or the banker? To which there is no right or wrong answer, and many of us will differ on our selection. One can argue it depends on your demographic; younger generations may choose the banker as they want to build a business and make money, however many rather choose the fisherman for his perspective, family values, and simplicity. Whatever way you look at it, the key lesson is to value balance and moderation in life, to enjoy the simple pleasures while you can, and at the same time find a stimulating purpose to keep you engaged!

JUST DO IT

One of the best job interview questions I have been asked is to talk about a concept you believe in that goes against the grain. For me, I often talk about the recruitment industry, as I believe if you know what job and firm you want to work, why not apply to them directly and let them know you exist, rather than going through an agent. Research the firm you are interested in based on factors such as industry, culture, potential fit, career trajectory, and location etc. As I see it, for a motivated self-starter, why would anyone use a recruiter to find a job? For those of you who may not be aware, a firm with two identical candidates in front of them with precisely the same experience and education profile except one came via a recruiter while the second reached out directly, will hire the direct candidate the majority of the time because they will be 25% cheaper on average after accounting for the recruitment firm fee. Another potential reason is the second candidate showed a proactive, hustling spirit to get to the interview in the first place!

Some people will always argue reaching out can be embarrassing as we naturally fear rejection, and that cold calling is a numbers game with a low chance of success. That's true however, I would always counter that the worst any employer can say is no, and if anything, they will respect you all the more for trying. As I see it, these are the hard yards outside our comfort zone we must face up to in order to make strides, and I am a big believer that the success of any person can be measured by the number of difficult conversations one is willing to have. Don't get me wrong, I continue to experience rejections all the time using this approach; however, I tend not to give up and I like to think that I can learn from each of my setbacks, often tweaking emails and opening lines to help me improve the process. Most importantly, I never take failure personally, and that's the key in my view. When you start to take it personally, it will affect you mentally and you will ultimately cave in and give up on yourself.

SET THE BAR EARLY

One theory I feel has some truth is that the money you earn in your 20s determines the money you earn in your 30s, which in turn determines the money you earn in your 40s and beyond. In other words, on average, your career foundation will impact your trajectory and earnings potential into the future. By foundation, I'm talking about your education profile, extracurricular activities, internships, part time jobs, and other interests. As Mark Twain once remarked, 'find a job you enjoy doing, and you will never have to work a day in your life'. The longer you procrastinate and skip from one post to another without purpose, the more likely you will negatively impact your deferred earnings in my view. I'm not suggesting it's impossible to turn your situation around, on the contrary there are many billionaires out there including Jack Ma (the founder of Alibaba) who did not set up until his late 40s, however on average the longer you wait the lower your chances of success. I would also argue that one's ability to hustle can be very advantageous in all walks of life, not just related to work, and is something that can be practiced and engrained over time through purposeful, deliberate action.

THE 3 Ps APPROACH

To take the job search a step further, there is no doubt that going through the process of searching for a job is never easy and can be quite demoralising to be honest! I developed a framework '3 Ps approach' to help me overcome the challenge and to improve my focus on the process. The first is to be Proactive, the second is

Persistence, and the third is to stay Positive as I will explain.

PROACTIVE – Step 1 is getting on top of the position you find yourself and fully understanding where the opportunities may present themselves. This includes researching thoroughly the jobs market in your niche area, putting together a list of prospective firms, studying their recent business activities, knowing who to contact, and working out their business email address. While this may sound intimidating, it really isn't and it helps to focus the mind on how badly you want the job. I also find spending time researching each company helps you determine whether you are truly passionate about their culture, ethos, and mission statement. For example, you may discover a firm pays really well or offers great maternity leave, however upon digging deeper and reading blogs about the company's culture, you learn they have a high staff turnover rate and really poor morale. Proactive also involves sending out 3 to 5 emails every morning to prospective employers, perhaps even personally writing to some by hand in order to emphasis just how interested you are. I know from my own experience that applying via their official careers website can often take a long time to even get a reply, and very often your application goes entirely unread. In my view, it is a much better approach to get in touch with the respective hiring manager directly who, in the worst-case scenario, will ignore your email, and in the best case may invite you in for an interview! As we now know from human behaviour, it is much harder to say 'no' to somebody when they reach out directly, so make it difficult for them to reject you – stack the odds in your favour where possible!

PERSISTENT - The second P is to be Persistent. Many prospective employers will put you on the long finger, and often may not even take the time to reply to your solicitation. The test here in my view is to persist. If you don't hear back from somebody after 1 week, follow up with another gentle reminder email or phone call. Don't assume the worst and take it personally. Remember that people are busy, and very often it is completely accidental that they don't get back to you. However, we all know how the mind works as we discussed earlier, and very often we convince ourselves that people are ignoring our emails and don't want to meet us for that coffee! In the vast majority of instances, this is not the case and following up with an email will give the recipient a nudge and the opportunity to prove it! In addition, sometimes a lack of reply can be a test of your resilience to see how badly you want it. Do you have the courage to follow up with another email or phone call? The easier option is to beat yourself up and accept defeat, however having the courage to follow up will immediately differentiate you from others, and likely push you into the 1% of candidates with the confidence to jump outside your comfort zone!

POSITIVE - Part of any job application process is rejection. Nobody is immune, and some of the most successful and wealthiest people on the planet have had the courage to admit they suffered lots of rejection and failure. Albert Einstein and Leonardo di Vinci come to mind as both struggled to find consistent work well into their 30s! Mark Cuban and Steve Jobs were fired from their jobs! It is really important to remain optimistic by nature and don't give up. Train your brain to stay positive in the face of adversity by putting things into perspective. Remember the worst they can say is no. Learn to set the bar low initially and adapt accordingly. For example, if you ask for an interview and they come back suggesting a coffee or video call instead, treat this as a major victory in your ability to write a credible introductory email or cold call. The nature of this high-risk strategy of taking your career into your own hands is that you are setting yourself up for lots of rejection along the journey! However, remember that you are also setting yourself up for putting your career under your control and taking ownership. Over the long term this will yield dividend both in terms of working for companies whom you respect and enjoy, but also expanding your network and largely winning the respect of others for your courage and audacity to make contact with strangers in the first place. Remember, while you may face 99% rejections, all it takes is 1 positive reply and subsequent job offer to make the whole effort so rewarding! Howard Schultz, the visionary behind Starbucks, received close to 240 rejections before he found somebody to take a risk and invest in his idea, and look how he ended up!

THE CV

The CV represents your gateway to a new job as it is often the only opportunity you have to present your case. With this in mind, the overall length of your CV should be no more than one page on average. Nobody is too important to extend beyond the one-page mark, unless you are an academic and have written research papers in my view!

The main reason for this is that the hiring manager has limited time and interest in reading through your profile. In fact, the average time a hiring manager spends reading through a CV is just 20 seconds according to various research findings, so make sure you have your key highlights clearly displayed front and centre!

The CV should also be tailored to the specific role you are applying for, by displaying relevant work experience and using appropriate action words to describe your responsibilities. For example, if you are applying for a creative role, make sure you use action words such as 'designed, created, originated, invented, crafted' etc. If you are applying for an experienced finance role, highlight your attention to detail, analysis skills, and ability with numbers! If you are applying for a graduate sales manager position, include your summer job as a restaurant manager because many of the same skills are transferrable in terms of leading people, speaking directly with customers, and perhaps managing budgets or complaints!

In addition, ensure your CV stands out by structuring your page into 3 sections including Professional, Education, and Interests. Professional should focus on your strongest and most relevant work experience starting with the most recent, and include key responsibilities, achievements, budget managed, and profit targets if applicable. Education should include all interesting qualifications including bachelor, masters, certificates, and diplomas. Include any relevant scores and awards which may boost your chances of separating yourself from the crowd. Finally, the Interests section is your opportunity to show the hiring manager what you like to do in your spare time and what makes you tick. This is the place to highlight your sporting, musical, or literary success along with any societies, clubs, charities, and other passions you enjoy. This is where you can really differentiate yourself from others, particularly if you have managed to excel in a particular field. Employers like to see that you have quirky interests and are curious in your spare time so don't be shy about that stamp collection or dance class!

As a final word on the CV, be sure to spend the necessary time on formatting such as font, spacing, and grammar as this is your self-portrait as far as the hiring manager is concerned. People often say that what you wear is more important than what you say in an interview; treat the CV as how you dress yourself, and without dressing smart you won't get in the door to start with! Then, if you do manage to get in the door, you only have a 20 second window to make a strong impression!

THE INTERNSHIP

I started my professional work experience with an accounting firm internship. I know many of you are interested in the accounting firms so I want to touch on my experience for what it's worth. I applied to one of the 'big 4' firms as part of their competitive 'Ace the business case' competition, from which they selected graduates for the summer internship program. The shortlisted 25 candidates were randomly split into 5 teams of 5 and invited to compete in an Apprentice style competition, whereby we were presented with a Harvard Business Review case study of a struggling company looking to survive in a certain industry. Each team prepared an analysis of the financial ratios, management capability, and wider industry viability assessment, before presenting to a group of firm partners and HR representatives the following day. While my team and I did not win the competition, I was awarded the best speaker and managed to attain an internship through the back door!

I was deployed into the Consumer & Industry Markets audit team which was a great opportunity to learn about some of the inner workings of the largest firms in the country. Clearly, I was coming in as a lowly summer intern and not exactly expected to revolutionise the client experience, or to bring in new streams of revenue over the 3 months! The work itself was varied and highly team focused, which was nice for me as the rookie. I found it dovetailed well with many of the same skills required on the sports field such as effective communication, discipline, and hard work! Like any job, parts of it were quite repetitive in terms of the printing and archiving of client files, but I guess you have to start somewhere! However, other parts were really interesting such as building the client audit file from start to finish, and taking ownership of the bank reconciliations which forms a key part of the audit review process. Other aspects of the role included proof reading, research, and ratio analysis, along with getting involved with the social committee!

While none of the tasks were particularly challenging in their own right, they did require lots of attention to detail and a strong commitment to ensure a high standard. In other words, they were putting my soft skills to the test as opposed to any technical accounting knowledge. In fact, I would argue the key to converting the internship into a full-time offer is to demonstrate your soft skills well, such as leadership, team-work, empathy, and communication ability, as opposed to the raw accounting flair which anyone can learn with experience!

Overall the firm made a really strong effort to progress the interns into full time graduate hires in my experience, which makes sense given they are investing significant resources into facilitating your summer internship in the first place! However, it is equally important that you use the opportunity to your advantage by weighing up whether you can see yourself flourishing in the role and committing the next 3 to 5 years minimum. In my case, the experience was really worthwhile as I learned there may be other careers for me, albeit I really wanted to gain the professional qualification as a grounding!

ECONOMICS 101

When I was graduating from university 10 years ago, investment banking was all the rage and graduates were jumping over each other to get an interview spot. I graduated in the midst of the global financial crisis of 2007/08 in one of the worst affected European countries, and so it was quite challenging to land a full-time job to be honest! While the domestic accounting firms were still running their graduate schemes, I was reading economics and opportunities were few and far between outside of academia. I eventually managed to gain an internship with an investment house as a research analyst which was great, and afforded me the opportunity to put my studies to work. The role allowed me to gain a sense for how the investment industry operates, and I managed to get exposure to many sides of the business including equity research, economics, sales, trading, and even corporate finance. Economics was my favourite as I felt like it underpinned every other business unit and the team at the time were working on some really interesting projects related to the aftermath of the financial crisis, such as the housing crisis, retail sales, and national GDP forecasts. One of my tasks was to monitor travel congestion indicators as a benchmark for economic growth which was interesting. Each morning there was a market update meeting with senior professionals in the firm and invariably all of the questions would be directed toward the economics team for guidance. I felt like this was the centre of the universe and really wanted to join the team!

THE MILK ROUND

The only difficulty was that these roles typically went to PhD level economists and data scientists rather than fresh university graduates still wet behind the ears! As a result, my mentor at the time advised me to apply to the investment banking graduate schemes in the UK. I felt like this was easy for him to suggest, and that it would be impossible for me to get a place on such an elite program, competing with Oxford and Cambridge graduates who typically filled such places. Despite the obvious challenges, I started applying to all the major banks as I felt they would be hiring the most candidates (safety in numbers!), and after countless rejections, I finally managed to gain an invitation to interview, which felt like a small reward for all the persistence and late-night application forms along the way!

COMPETENCY BASED INTERVIEW

The interview itself was a standard 'competency based' interview over the phone. These are common across the banks, accounting practices, and law firms, and especially competitive in the investment banking field. The interviewer asked me a range of questions such as 1) give an example of leadership and how you motivated a team to achieve something, 2) share a setback and what you learned from it, 3) discuss one of your main weaknesses and how you have overcome it, 4) how would your friends describe you, 5) why should we hire you instead of the other candidates knocking on the door. These are tough questions to answer under pressure so let me detail the tips I learned to frame your response!

You can prepare in advance for 90% of the competency-based questions so you can have examples to hand for each of the questions, however try to avoid using the same response twice! Under the pressures of the interview on the day, your mind will go blank which makes it extra important to prepare well in advance. Reflect on your university experience and extracurricular activities to come up with a list of highlights which may be relevant in the interview. For example, perhaps you were captain of the debating team, played a key position on the sports field, or were part of a very successful musical choir. All of these achievements are very relevant to the interview and should be highlighted where possible. Structure your answers to include all of these activities so that your example of a teamwork experience could include your end of term class presentation, leadership may be your society representative role in university, and communication may include your public speaking competition. Ensure you have a good narrative to explain each of the core competency angles that may be examined on the day, and try to demonstrate your best self in the process!

In addition, always end each question on a positive note. If you are asked to share a weakness or an example of where you failed at something, don't just share the example, instead turn it into a positive story. For example, let's imagine your answer to the weakness question is that you tend to overanalyse things, struggle to delegate responsibilities, or are ultra-competitive at inappropriate times. These are all potentially fatal weaknesses in certain circumstances, and so you have to back yourself up on where you have identified tools to improve each limitation. If you tend to overanalyse at times, talk about what you have done to overcome this weakness. Perhaps you have learned to take a step back and look at the problem from a top-down perspective using a new toolset you developed. There is no doubt we all make mistakes, however try to separate yourself from the crowd by demonstrating that you not only have the ability to learn from your mistakes, but you can also turn them into a positive outcome as this is what the interviewer is interested in!

The final stage of the interview preparation is to thoroughly research the firm you are interviewing with. I would argue this may be the most important, yet widely overlooked part of the interview. The majority of candidates walk into the interview believing they have great education and work experience, and are confident that their credentials will do the talking! While this may be the case for some, for the rest of us including myself, this may be the part of the interview where we can differentiate ourselves by putting in the research hours. The interviewer is well aware that each candidate has likely applied to 10 other firms at the same time (which is a good thing to hedge your bets and also for the interview experience!), and as a result may wish to understand why the candidate has applied to this particular firm. To this question, I believe a couple of differentiating factors can help you stand out, such as studying the sponsorship programs of the firm, knowing their mission statement, history, management team, and core values. For example, a passion for sport may help at HSBC given they sponsor the Wimbledon Championships and other golf tournaments, while an interest in music may suit Bank of America as they are associated with the Chicago Symphony Orchestra. Knowing these interests and using them to your advantage can help you rise above other candidates and swing the interview in your favour. In addition, you should know high level facts of the firm such as the CEO and management team by name, number of employees and corporate headquarters, the various business units and geographic focus, along with relevant news and any recent corporate activity. For example, if you are interviewing at Fitbit, it may help to know that they are in the process of being acquired by Google! This is basic information widely available online and relevant to your interview whether you realise it or not. Once I got beyond the interview stage, I was invited to attend an all-expenses paid 'Assessment Centre' which was to take place in London!

THE ASSESSMENT CENTRE

The assessment centre was an incredible experience. Flying to London by myself for the 24-hour trip felt like an episode of Dragon's Den and I can still remember preparing my notes and interview answers on the flight over. It was a 7am start in the bank headquarters which in hindsight I think was the first test to see if any of us students slept in! The day was split into 2 parts; the morning session was focused on numeracy, written tests, and a case study, followed by an afternoon of extensive one-on-one interviews and a short team presentation. Throughout the day, it was clear that I was being assessed at every juncture and interaction, both with representatives from the bank along with my fellow applicants. The whole purpose of the day is for the bank to get to know you, and to understand what makes you tick. There were 12 candidates including myself at this particular assessment day and all were from top UK universities such as Oxford, Cambridge, and Warwick. I felt way out of my depth and struggled through the morning session, however I felt ok after the case study and presentation. I also had eight individual interviews, each one focused on a core competency such as leadership, communication, setbacks, and risk-taking, and I felt pretty good coming out of the majority. I flew back that night and to my surprise, received a phone call the following week with the positive news!

THE GRADUATE PROGRAM

I joined the graduate scheme in August 2011 with 180 international graduates from all parts of the world who would be posted to one of the bank's international offices. It was a fantastic way to build a network of new colleagues and fellow bankers from all walks of life who were embarking on the same exciting journey. I made some great friends and many of whom I am still in touch with, which was one of the big advantages of such a large program. Overall, it was a 2-year graduate scheme and I rotated across 3 different business units, namely sales, portfolio analysis, and macro strategy. Each was very different and gave me an opportunity to both learn about various parts of the bank and build the relevant skills!

The sales role mainly involved preparing pitchbooks on marketing the investment products, conducting competitor analysis of certain products, meeting with clients, along with creating a lot of tables and charts on Excel! The portfolio construction team was a more technical role focused on assessing investment risk across asset classes in terms of understanding the country level risk, industry risk, currency risk, and concentration risk of each individual portfolio. In addition, the team was responsible for stress testing portfolio performance against shocks to the financial system such as the 2007/08 global financial crisis, SARS, and The Great Depression. I spent a lot of time on Excel between interacting directly with the investment teams and portfolio managers to better understand their risk exposure.

The third and final role of my graduate scheme was with the macro strategy team, and was the rotation I pushed hard for from the outset. This unit was part of the investment team and responsible for assessing ongoing macro and policy related events, along with communicating investment implications directly to institutional and retail clients of the bank. Certain examples of events I focused on during my time on the desk included the US and German elections, the Venezuelan oil crisis, and global monetary policy measures. In addition, the head of the team travelled constantly to meet with clients, and so as the junior member of the team, I was tasked with updating his various presentations and preparing slides as required! It was a really interesting role and a great way for me to gain a top-down macroeconomic understanding of four asset classes namely equities, fixed income, currencies, and commodities. However, I was most interested in the commodity markets and really wanted to gain a granular understanding of the oil market in particular.

COMMODITY TRADING

After 2 years at the bank, I managed to secure a job at a commodity firm where my role was the crude oil trading analyst. After 12 lengthy interviews, I was excited to join the team and was responsible for the desk's fundamental analysis efforts of the global crude oil market. Initially I was tasked with building spreadsheet models related to supply and demand balances, vessel tracking, refinery margins, and refinery maintenance schedules which was very interesting and gave me a solid introduction to the oil market. Later I moved into a direct trading seat which allowed me the opportunity to put money where my mouth was. I learned a lot about the psychology of trading, in particular managing my emotions on the job!

After four years in the role, an opportunity presented itself to join a start-up trading desk backed by a larger entity. I was very excited to land the job and promptly relocated to the Middle East for a couple of years where the role was based. I discovered a whole new culture and way of life to be honest! The role itself involved physically moving oil cargoes from producing to consuming countries, which was quite a big responsibility given the sums of money involved, and at the same time working with government entities in all parts of the world. I learned a great deal both on the job in terms of diplomacy, and also the cultural emphasis in certain countries on investing in long term relationships for mutual commercial success. There was also a reasonable amount of travel in order to develop and foster relations with clients face to face. After two enjoyable years, I relocated back to the UK where I secured a role in the often-volatile airline and producer hedging business.

MIND THE VOLATILITY

Reflecting on my career, I have moved into increasingly niche firms and specific roles which I think is quite natural for most professions. Over time, I have developed quite a broad experience ranging from the macro strategist and oil analyst, to the financial and physical oil trading, and more recently to the focus on client hedging. However, with the impact of Covid-19, it has really hit home that I am working in a volatile sector of the economy! Unlike a lawyer, accountant, or teacher who generally enjoy a consistent flow of work, as an oil professional, you are subject to the wild swings of the economic peaks and troughs! In the good times when oil prices are high, companies are investing in exploration and production projects, and jobs are abundant in hubs such as Scotland, Canada, and the Middle East. However, in the bad times, and unfortunately there have been a number of bad times over the past decade, jobs are slashed and incomes suffer for obvious reasons!

While my career has weathered most of the more cyclical parts of the oil industry as I have been on the trading side, I recently joined a bank in an energy trading role focused on serving clients such as the airlines and producers. As we now know, the airlines have been among the worst affected by Covid-19 which has put a halt to global travel. When the airlines are moving, they need to hedge their oil price and banks are typically responsible for providing the liquidity necessary to mitigate the price risk of daily fluctuations. When you think about it, airlines spend on average 80% of their total costs buying jet fuel, and so if an airline can effectively manage their oil price cost base, they can save huge sums of money and perhaps even pass on these savings to holiday-makers!

My point is that we are all susceptible to economic shocks such as a pandemic, and as a result, we should be mindful of the industries and sectors we build the foundations of our career and earnings potential around. For example, starting a career in the oil or coal industry today may not be the best long-term choice given the government incentives and momentum around the The Paris

Agreement to move away from such energy sources. Equally, starting a career right now in the hospitality, restaurant, traditional high-street retail, co-working space, and leisure companies, may prove challenging!

THE EXPAT

I have lived overseas for my entire career to date. So many of us decide to live abroad for at least a couple of years after graduation, and I think there are some great benefits to doing so! While many decide to do it for a gap-year, a graduate scheme, or lifestyle factors, I also feel there is so much to be gained from an independence, curiosity, and cultural perspective. To be clear, travel works for some people, while for others, getting outside their comfort zone is too difficult. My own view is that it is healthy to get outside of your familiar bubble for a while (if you are fortunate enough to be in a position to do so), and the sooner you can do it, the earlier you can benefit from it! So many of us find love on our travels, make friends for life, or even have a light bulb moment for a business idea while travelling!

Admittedly my story was slightly less glamorous, initially moving to London for work as mentioned earlier, and still here 10 years later! In my case, it was quite an eye opener moving to a city with a population three times greater than the whole country I came from! I didn't know a single person in the city at the time, and I moved the day before I was due to start my first day on the job! I rented short-term student accommodation for the first couple of weeks to settle in, and found myself sharing a kitchen and single bathroom with 8 to 10 people! I remember discussing with family before boarding the flight that I was treating the adventure as a two-year plan, and I would then move back home. However, the career opportunities were very good and I soon found myself really enjoying the lifestyle. Admittedly, I was lucky to join a structured two-year graduate program with so many like-minded graduates to hang out with!

After close to 7 years in London, I decided to pursue a fairly unique opportunity in the Middle East as discussed earlier. This was a difficult decision on a personal level as I built a life and relationship in London, and enjoyed the city and proximity to my family. However, I felt approaching my late 20s, this may be my last opportunity to travel extensively again, and so I managed to convince myself to give it a go! It was a great experience both from a professional and personal perspective. I initially lived in Dhahran, along the eastern province of Saudi Arabia, and enjoyed the great restaurants and friendly people! I wanted to live close to the office for the first 6 months, before moving to Bahrain which is a beautiful small island rich in culture and activities – if you are contemplating a move to the region please do get in touch!

SOFT SKILLS

I want to finish this chapter by spending a little more emphasis on soft skills as they really are so important. The science shows that young people who enjoy an extracurricular activity (such as music, acting, scouts, and sports) show a higher propensity to advance in life both in terms of career and family. For me, this makes sense given that so much of any success is based on the soft skills practiced such as emotional intelligence, judgement, and commitment, rather than the technical knowledge alone. For example, our ability to read emotions without direct communication, and our judgement of when to say and do the right thing, are just a couple of core soft skills that can make all the difference in certain situations.

As it relates to our purposeful work, employers confirmed in a recent survey that a degree alone is no longer enough to secure a top job, which explains why universities are investing resources into societies and clubs to help students bolster their credentials. In fact, many universities have created a co-curriculum to include part-time work and volunteering, societies and student clubs, and sports, on top of the academic curriculum to better equip students. This is a welcome addition as we now know the premium employers place on such activities. Think about the opportunity cost for students participating in co-curricular activities; for many it is watching television, nights out, or playing video games. Now more than ever, thriving in university is about the student taking initiative and firm control over their curriculum and time allocation.

Interestingly, many high school classes run interactive questionnaires among students to vote on their peer 'most likely to succeed in life', and surprisingly, recent studies suggest the results may be a reliable indicator of financial and educational attainment later in life. Without question, students are taking into consideration more than just academics when contemplating their peer's future success. They are also assessing soft skills such as emotional intelligence, leadership, communication, and teamwork among others. One such US survey showed that teachers who rated their students as having strong interpersonal skills, work rate, and regular participation in extracurricular activities, were much more likely to achieve a well-rounded life over the following decade. Of course, certain roles place a premium on academic excellence (don't think you will get a job in NASA with strong leadership alone!), however the point is achievements outside the classroom are often equally important, and the landscape is rapidly evolving.

QUOTES ON PURPOSE

'It is not enough to have lived. We should be determined to live for something' – Winston Churchill

'People take different roads seeking fulfillment and happiness. Just because they are not on your road doesn't mean they've gotten lost' – Dalai Lama

'Efforts and courage are not enough without purpose and direction' – John F. Kennedy

'The best way to lengthen out our days is to walk steadily and with a purpose' – Charles Dickens

'Try not to become a man of success but rather try to become a man of value' – Albert Einstein

PART VIII

MONEY

A CLEAR PLAN

In this section I want to focus on the economics of pensions, property, and saving accounts among other money considerations.

THE PENSION

Traditionally, pensions have been so complex and difficult to understand that most people delegate responsibility to a seasoned 'professional'. In a basic test of financial literacy, the average person answers slightly more than 1 out of 5 questions correctly, and the vast majority of people worry they won't have enough for retirement. With this in mind, there is arguably no more important money topic to get your head around than the personal pension plan. This is your tax-efficient piggy bank to enjoy a worry-free retirement, and the reality is that the sooner you start utilising it, the earlier you can enjoy the fruits of your hard labour. In the UK for example, the average pension pot is slightly over £60,000 according to the FCA (Financial Conduct Authority), which while it sounds like a lot, equates to an income of just £2,500 per year, and when combined with the state allowance still falls below minimum wage (albeit the data does not include those who have multiple pension pots and those collecting buy-to-let property income). In addition, only 1 in 8 people have a pension pot exceeding £250,000, which is the recommended minimum amount required to retire, based on government data. I want to share with you the few rules I learned from others on the subject including the importance of, 1) Starting early, 2) Diversification and 3) Understand the small print.

STARTING EARLY - Pensions are there to help you. Most employers offer generous schemes to encourage you to start contributing into a tax efficient pension. In fact, many of them will match your contribution up to 8% of your monthly pay-check, which means you are effectively receiving 'free money' further down the road by participating in such schemes! Due to the effect of compounding, the earlier you start contributing a regular fixed amount such as $50 per month, the more funds you will have to enjoy later in life. I started my own pension when I was 22 years old fresh out of university. I now have a small sum invested with one low cost provider, which means I can easily keep track of my pot, and avail of lower fees from having it pooled together (some people have multiple pension with various former employers which can end up being quite complex to manage). At the time when I started my pension, one had to manually opt-in as there was no automatic enrollment policy, however automatic enrollment has since been introduced across many countries following behavioural economics study findings. These science-based initiatives showed that the average person does want to delay gratification and participate into a pension, but is unlikely to do so because they feel intimidated by their complexity. It is difficult to overestimate how significant a role this seemingly minor automatic pension enroll adjustment can play in our long-term financial wellbeing from a public policy perspective.

Another important consideration into the motivations for starting early is the simple fact that we are all living longer on average, and so the need for retirement savings has never been greater. In addition, companies are no longer offering the more generous 'defined benefit' pension which is based on a percentage of final salary (typically two thirds of the final salary before retirement), and are instead providing 'defined contribution' pension schemes whereby the investment risk lies exclusively with the employee. The reason for this change is very simple; traditional defined benefit pension schemes are very expensive to run and companies can no longer afford to pay them out. As a result, the millennial generation is now stuck with stomaching the volatility of stock markets which is a challenge by itself during recent times!

DIVERSIFICATION - Diversification is a critical recipe for a successful retirement strategy. As the old maxim goes 'don't put all your eggs in one basket', whether it be property, shares, or other assets. The easiest way to build a diversified pension pot is to firstly start allocating a small percent of your monthly pay into a balanced portfolio of Exchange Traded Funds (ETFs) and index trackers. An ETF is an instrument used to invest in a basket of securities which usually track an underlying benchmark such as the S&P 500 or FTSE 100. I began by picking some of the largest national companies across airlines, banks, and consumer staples, and then putting a small amount of money to work. It was among the best learning curves as I suddenly started reading the business newspapers in order to keep tabs on the share prices! Unfortunately, I quickly found myself in the red, after one of my stocks was nationalised (talk about bad luck because this very rarely happens!), while some of the other names halved in value over the next 12 months following the 2007/08 financial crisis. The positive takeaway was that I still carry these scars today, and that I now understand the banks and other 'certainties' are not necessarily as safe as we think!

Another solid way to diversify your capital and build a nest egg is to get on the property ladder in my view. Easier said than done I know, but the rational is that we all have to pay the rent anyway, so you might as well be paying down your own mortgage and capital instead. This doesn't mean you should take out an interest free mortgage for 25 years. On the contrary, try to pay back as much interest and capital as possible in order to avoid facing a big bill further down the road! While the property itself may not be glamorous for the majority of us, that's really not point and the fact is that we all have to start somewhere! Whether it be a former council flat, an apartment in a neighbouring commuter town, or an old property badly in need of some TLC, at least this is your asset, and over the long term you can work to repay the debt and build up some equity for your pension in the process!

Other strategies include regularly putting some money into a designated pension fund, whether actively or passively managed. By actively managed, we imply a professional investor with relevant expertise will manage our money, and make appropriate investing decisions in terms of timing and asset allocation on our behalf. On the other hand, passively managed is the cheaper option as your fund will track a range of market benchmarks without the market timing and tactical portfolio rebalancing. We will touch on this in greater detail later when we talk about fees. However, the immediate point here is that specific funds may give you exposure to certain sectors, demographics, and countries whose story you believe in over the medium to long term. For example, many of us believe in the emerging markets in terms of future economic growth potential, and at a sector level many are excited about the future of robotics, automation, and digital currency! On this basis, we can build our pension fund around these investment themes so we have exposure to them playing out!

UNDERSTAND THE SMALL PRINT - The third point I want to highlight to the fees. This is arguably the most important factor to note as from my understanding, the vast majority of people don't know what fees they are paying! While we all know to hand the cost of our monthly rent, mortgage, or car loan, very few of us know what rate we are paying on our pension despite it often being a multiple of the other expenses. This is not our fault and is more to do with the transparency of the provider, and the way information is presented (or not). As a result, like any industry where producers have an information advantage over consumers, prices can get out of whack very quickly.

In my opinion, these fees are more important than the actual investment return over the long term. For example, over 20 years and based on a pension pot of £150,000, the difference between a 1% annual management fee and a 2% annual management fee is almost £60,000. Similarly, the life-time charge on a £1million pension pot over 25 years ranges from about £300,000 to £850,000 depending on whether you opt to manage the portfolio yourself or hire an advisor to do it for you. With this in mind, what is a competitive annual fee to pay? As always, it depends on the service you enjoy, whether you want a fully managed service with all the bells and whistles, or a self-service offering. For the fully managed service, you can expect to pay between 2% and 3% per annum on average, while the self-service option is cheaper and should range from about 0.8% to 1.2% annually. Exact fees will depend on the average investment size (some platforms offer economies of scale in reduced fees above an initial investment of say £50,000 or £100,000), and any preference for environmentally friendly portfolios for those who would like to invest in companies with a strong sustainability focus or Environmental, Social, & Governance (ESG) score.

To use another example, assume you invest £10,000 over 40 years with no fees and with an average annual investment return of 7%. Over the 40 years, this will return slightly over £140,000. However, by introducing a seemingly slight 2% annual investment charge, your returns will drop by about £75,000 to just £65,000. By replacing the 2% charge with 0.5%, returns increase to £120,000 after the same 40-year period. While there are many other charges in the small print (such as entry and exit costs, execution fees, spread costs etc.), the annual investment charge is the most important fee to understand in terms of portfolio impact, and keeping it as lean as possible can help maximise the value of your hard-earned pension pot over the long term. The easiest way to reduce the fee, in my view, is to ensure your money is put to work in a low cost, efficient manner. It should come as little surprise that the vast majority of major pension providers and asset managers are fully aware that the public are not exactly fully in the loop when it comes to fees, and so they can build in an extra margin for themselves, keeping all the additional charges hidden in the small print!

In fact, I recently scanned the websites of the main pension funds, and found that the vast majority do not share their fees and charges in an upfront, easy to understand way. By contrast, when you go shopping for a mortgage you can quickly compare vendor products by looking at all factors such as duration, interest rate, upfront charges, and initial term on a transparent, easy to use platform. However, this simple frame of reference doesn't exist in the pension world to my knowledge, and fees such as platform, investment fund, execution, market spread, and exit fees often aren't even mentioned in the product details, despite adding up to over 1% in some cases, on top of the annual management charge! It often reminds me of the banks and foreign exchange dealers on the high street who advertise as 0% commission, despite building in as much as 20% margin in the conversion rate bid-offer spread they offer you in-store!

With this in mind, I believe it is best to put your money to work in a low-cost platform that will invest in low-cost funds called ETFs and index funds, as opposed to investing in the well-known, star fund manager names. While the big star manager names work well for some, they tend to have a couple of great years of performance before imploding or underperforming the market for a sustained period, according to the studies. As a result, I personally feel much more comfortable investing in a product that will simply track an index whether it be an equity, bond, or even a commodity benchmark. These securities then invest in a basket of names which fit the category of product I choose to invest. For example, if I want exposure to large capitalisation US equities, I may choose to invest in an S&P 500 ETF which will replicate the performance of the underlying stock market. As a general rule, these securities as a portfolio should be global diversified, highly liquid, and low cost with strong correlation to their stated underlying benchmarks.

Interestingly, more and more employees are opting to make their own pension decisions without consulting with a financial advisor, at least partially due to the fees associated with hiring help! In a recent FCA survey for example, close to 50% of retirees decided themselves whether to receive their pension 25% tax-free lump sum, take a drawdown, or purchase an annuity. The most common pension withdrawal rate last year was 8%, meaning for every £10,000 you saved into your pension pot, you received £800 per year. This percentage is definitely on the high side given the average person will live about 20 years (and rising in line with longevity trends) after they reach 65 years. A more sustainable rate would be 4-5% per year, and some experts would argue even this drawdown is on the high side too! For the lucky few with larger pension pots exceeding £1m, the average drawdown is closer to 2-4% per year which is far more sustainable.

RISK APPETITE

The first exercise to complete when setting up a pension or investment portfolio is to understand your risk profile. There are lots of free resources online to do this, and it is good practice and well worthwhile. Everyone has a slightly different risk appetite (depending on factors such as age and stage in life, as well as personalised ability to ride out the storms in the short term, in order to make bigger gains over the long term), and this is why tailoring a portfolio is critical as we all have a unique attitude to risk. As an example, people with a risk tolerance of 1/5 will prioritise avoiding losses at all costs and as such their portfolios will be heavily overweight short maturity developed market government bonds, as well as money market instruments. Their motivation will be to maximise consistent income, while at the same time preserving capital. On the contrary, individual portfolios with higher risk appetite of 4/5 will be concentrated in developed market equities and higher yielding risk assets such as emerging market equities, corporate bonds, and commodities. People in this higher risk category are deemed comfortable taking risk, and willing to ride out the market fluctuations in order to produce long term bigger gains. Projected returns over the long term will range on average from +3% to +5% (based on historical data) depending on tolerance to risk and fees!

INVESTMENT PERFORMANCE

I believe many of us massively overcomplicate the art of investing by stressing over which fund we should invest in or who we want to look after our money. Instead, we should focus on the theme of 'fee minimisation' as over the long term many of these similar funds will perform in a similar manner. Think about it, whether we invest in a UK equity fund managed by a star fund manager or a UK equity index fund which tracks the benchmark performance, investment performance will be similar over the long term, yet fees will be significantly lower in the latter option. As Princeton University professor Burton Malkiel claimed in his 1970s bestselling book A Random Walk Down Wall Street, 'a blindfolded monkey throwing darts at a newspaper's financial pages could select a portfolio that would do just as well as one carefully selected by experts'. In fact, a subsequent study had 100 monkeys do just that by throwing darts at the financial pages each year from 1964 to 2010, and the results showed the stocks they landed on beat the experts 98% of the time! Rather than stock selection, the more important consideration is asset allocation and understanding the level of volatility you are comfortable taking. Once you determine this, you can then rebalance your portfolio on a quarterly or annual basis, based on individual fund performance and the wider economy!

One certainty is that the market will go through phases of uncertainty and gyrations. In my view, the best place to put your money in these times is to leave it exactly where it is! There is little point in trying to become a maverick by timing the market during unprecedented market volatility such as Covid-19, when nobody knows how it will play out! For example, if you had your money invested in the markets prior to Covid-19 and now see a 20 to 30% decline in your assets, try to avoid making rash decisions. Instead, sit tight, don't panic, and have faith in history. In addition, and contrary to what most people believe, I think one should continue to invest in the market if you have a regular monthly investment process, as this can be a great strategy to weather extreme volatility and benefit from dollar-cost averaging (avoiding the market highs and lows by dividing your overall investment into a period of time). Of course, if your circumstances have changed (ill-health, lost job, or reduced hours), then it makes sense to divest a portion of your investment into an easy access savings account as needed.

BRICKS AND MORTAR

For most of us, buying a property is likely the largest investment of our lifetime, and all the more so today when you consider the sustained rise in property prices combined with wage stagnation. In fact, across most major cities the ratio of outright property prices to income has never been higher, reaching 15x in some cases despite mortgage lending caps typically around 4.5x wages. In other words, it has become practically impossible for one to afford a property without winning the lottery, or inheriting a lot of money which of course for most of us is unrealistic! Despite this, getting onto the property ladder remains our single biggest financial motivation, according to many well-respected surveys. Taking this into account, lets discuss the process and necessary steps, along with some practical tips which I wish I had known!

PERSONAL - The most important step in the process is to thoroughly understand what you are looking to achieve. Firstly, ask yourself in depth about your stage in life, relationship status, family objectives, and aspirations in terms of proximity to work and commute time. Bear in mind, a very important component of one's overall happiness in life is commuting time, according to the happiness experts. Overall, this internal reflection should help to frame the foundation of your search in terms of understanding your own motives and vision for your future home. You should also try to extrapolate your likely position out 3-5 years minimum as the reality is that you are going to live in this property for some time!

FINANCIAL - This next step is to take into account your financial goals and aspirations as it relates to the property. Are you looking to purchase to create a home or a financial investment, or perhaps both? For those currently renting, the financial motivation is often to avoid the 'rent trap' i.e. paying so much money on rent that we can never set aside enough savings to get a foothold on the property ladder. However, the reality is that getting out of the rent trap has never been harder given the chunky deposits required, and to make matters worse, the cost of renting is often higher than the cost of paying off a mortgage on a monthly basis, thanks to the ultra-low interest rate environment!

In addition, it is prudent to evaluate your job prospects and whether you can afford to carry the weight of any setback either professionally or personally for a sustained period. Provision for various scenarios such as the possibility of losing your job and having no income for 3-6 months, ill-health, or a sharp increase in interest rates which would spike your monthly mortgage payments. While some would suggest it is unhealthy to look negatively on yourself, and instead to focus on the positives, the reality is you are engaging in a very significant undertaking not dissimilar to a marriage (many mortgage products are up to a 35 year commitment!), and so it is imperative you take an objective and unbiased approach to your investment decision in my view. Most personal finance experts advise saving at least 15-20% of your monthly pay check, keeping your rent around 30%, with the remainder going on discretionary outgoings. However, it makes sense to get that monthly savings rate as high as possible, and if you can approach 40% through short-term personal sacrifices, all the better for you!

LOCATION – For those who manage to get the finances in order, the next step is to identify a shortlist of preferred areas to live based on your personalised situation, and to map out in detail the pros and cons to each location. While you may feel like this is far too much homework and you simply want to put a roof over your head, remember this may be the largest investment of your life, and could make or break your retirement income! Reflection points should include whether you are looking for nice nearby amenities such as public transport connectivity, a local park, proximity to work or family, and quality schools, or perhaps you are looking to find a regeneration area which may help your property appreciate in value over time. Choose your location based on what suits you, and don't be drawn into peer and social pressures!

THE MORTGAGE PROCESS

I spent months reading books and websites about the intricacies of mortgage products. I still don't understand how anybody without a university degree can fully understand the products and make an informed decision! Let's discuss each component in turn so we are super clear on the process together.

INTEREST RATE - The first question to ask yourself is whether you want to pay a fixed or a floating rate of interest over the life cycle of your mortgage. As I see it, the main consideration is whether you want the certainty of knowing the interest rate you will pay, or feel comfortable taking an interest rate risk that may or may not move in your favour. For example, if interest rates decline over the life cycle of your floating rate mortgage, then you will save money as your floating rate will track the interest rate decline and capture the savings. However, if interest rates increase over the same period, you will pay out more money to the bank, in which case the fixed rate would prove the cheaper option. As a general rule, a variable rate mortgage makes sense in a falling interest rate or recessionary environment (generally speaking), while the fixed rate product makes sense when interest rates are moving higher. For those of you who don't feel comfortable committing to either product, you can also opt to have your mortgage fixed for a set period of time, before then moving onto a variable rate for the remainder of the duration. For example, one can commit to an initial 2-year fixed rate mortgage, and then move onto a variable rate for the remainder of the mortgage term. Alternatively, you can also choose a 3-year, 5-year, or 10-year fixed rate mortgage product, among others. As a guide, the longer the fixed term of the mortgage, the more confidence one should have that interest rates will rise above that committed to rate during that period of time, and visa-versa. Otherwise, it doesn't make financial sense to lock it in!

DURATION - The next consideration is to choose the appropriate mortgage duration. This refers to how many years you want the mortgage product to last, and typically ranges from 25 to 35 years. To be clear, this is the period of time you have to repay the mortgage product in full, including the interest component. The longer the duration, the lower the monthly interest payments will be because you are spreading it out over more months. However, on the flipside, the longer the duration, the more interest you will pay and the greater the profit margin for the lender. For example, let's assume you are borrowing $300,000 (property costs $330,000 and you put down a $30,000 deposit), at an interest rate of 2%, and you are weighing up whether to commit to a 25-year or 35-year mortgage duration. Let's run the numbers together to see the difference: over a 25-year mortgage term, you will make monthly repayments (including capital and interest) of $1,270 (interest component starts off at $500 per month and capital at $770), and will pay a total interest bill of $81,500, which on top of the $300,000 borrowing, brings the total cost over the life of the product to $381,500. For the 35-year duration product, using the same 2% interest rate and $300,000 borrowing, you will incur monthly repayments of $995 (interest starts at $500 and capital at $495), and will pay an interest bill of $117,300, on top of the $300,000 borrowing, bringing the total cost to $417,300. As you can see, while the 35-year option has cheaper monthly repayments, the overall cost of the product is 44% more expensive vs. the 25-year product. These are very real numbers and can have a massive impact on one's affordability and overall budget. While it's all well and good running the numbers together, clearly one's personal circumstances and affordability will dictate their choice of product duration.

DEPOSIT – The deposit consideration is pretty straightforward, as you either have it or you don't! However, there are a couple of useful tips worth taking into account. The minimum deposit typically required by the lender is 10%, unless you can benefit from a government scheme such as first-time buyer relief or needs-based support. For most people, 10% is the minimum deposit required, which means that in order to purchase a $300,000 property, you will need to put down $30,000 as a deposit, and the bank will lend you the rest. The technical term for this arrangement is called the Loan to Value (LTV), and in this scenario, you are looking for a 90% LTV mortgage, and contributing 10% out of pocket. Deposits typically move in increments of 5% so the next level of deposit would be 15%, then 20%, 25%, and so on. In general, the higher the deposit you can bring to the table, the lower the interest rate will be for the mortgage, and therefore the cheaper it is for you (excluding any opportunity cost). This makes sense given that the lower the deposit, the higher your risk of default from the lender perspective, particularly in the event of negative property prices or sustained higher interest rates over time. As a result, it is in your interest to put down the highest deposit you can afford within reason. It is worth noting however that the marginal cost saving to you of increasing your deposit declines as you go above a certain level. From my research, this level is about 15%; in other words, if you can get your deposit to 15% you will obtain a very competitive mortgage rate from a bank, provided you shop around and do the research! While a 10% deposit may achieve the mortgage you require, this is considered the entry level mortgage deposit nowadays and so the bank will not offer you a particularly competitive rate given you are still deemed a relatively high risk!

In fact, you should notice there is usually quite a significant interest rate differential between the 10% and 15% deposit. For example, right now in the highly competitive UK mortgage market for a 2-year fixed rate product, the 10% deposit rate (or 90% LTV) is about 2% while the 15% deposit rate (85% LTV) is about 1.6%. Taking a $300,000 property price as an example, a 10% deposit with an interest rate of 2% over a 30-year term will cost you a total of $89,000 in interest payments alone, while the 15% deposit at 1.6% will cost you a significantly lower $66,000 in total interest over the same 30 year period. For those of you fortunate enough to have a deposit base of greater than 15%, you will of course achieve a lower interest rate again, however from my analysis the interest differential between a 15% and 20% deposit is much less than the differential between a 10% and 15% deposit.

SMALL PRINT – While we have dealt with the core pillars of the mortgage process, it is really important to consider the finer details which can really add up if not fully taken into account. Terms such as the 'annual overpayment allowance' or 'early repayment charge' can make a big difference to your bottom line, yet are often overlooked as part of the decision-making process. The annual overpayment allowance refers to the amount you can overpay on your outstanding mortgage balance every year, and is typically capped at 10% for most high street banks. Any payment above this cap can incur early repayment charges as high as 5% of the outstanding balance in some cases so take notice!

In addition, evaluate any other charges in the small print such as a 'mortgage arrangement fee' which can typically range from $999 to $1,499 depending on the lender, along with a valuation fee of $150 to $400 which is often incurred by the bank. While these upfront fees are often avoidable by shopping around, the analysis suggests that it is generally cheaper to pay the upfront fee in order to benefit from a cheaper advertised rate (typically on promotion). Note that any upfront fee can usually be added to the overall mortgage balance, rather than having to pay it upfront in cash. For example, I see online at the time of writing that there is a 2-year fixed rate offer of 1.6% with a $999 mortgage arrangement fee, or alternatively a 2-year fixed rate of 1.75% with no arrangement fee. In order to determine the cheaper option, you can add the $999 onto the overall mortgage balance and calculate the interest due over the first 2-year fixed term. In this case, the 1.6% comes to a total of $8,311 in interest payments over the initial 2 years, while the 1.75% comes to a total of $9,058 over the same period, thereby making the first option cheaper by $700. The lesson here is simple: don't always be deceived by the off-putting upfront fees!

Also, take note of whether the lender is charging mortgage interest by the day, week, or month. While the vast majority charge by the day, it is worth double checking as this is where they really make their money (or where you can really save!). To put this in context, we often hesitate to buy a cup of coffee for $3, yet don't realise that our mortgage provider is often making $25-30 per day on our starter home mortgage because of the daily interest calculation they enjoy!

OVERPAYMENTS - Making regular overpayments on your mortgage can bring significant savings, and shave years off the mortgage term if you can afford to do it. Consistently overpaying can also make you eligible for better deals on remortgage rates when the time comes, as you may have a higher equity value on your property, thereby reducing the all-important LTV ratio we discussed earlier. Some banks will offer 'offset mortgages' whereby your mortgage account will be linked to your savings account and the interest charged on your outstanding mortgage balance will be the difference between the two accounts. For example, if you have an outstanding mortgage balance of $300,000 and $50,000 in your offset savings account, the mortgage interest will only be calculated on the difference between the two of $250,000. However, it is worth noting that these offset accounts typically come with a higher mortgage interest rate, and so it worth calculating the differential to determine whether the additional cost is worth the added benefit, taking into account your personal circumstances.

Let's work through a couple of examples of the overpayment impact on mortgage balances. Assume you have an outstanding mortgage balance of $250,000, a 25-year term mortgage, a 3.5% annual interest rate, and are trying to decide whether to overpay by $100 or $250 per month. If you decide to overpay $100 per month you will save slightly over $14,000 in interest charges over the 25-year period and the mortgage term would reduce from 25 years to 20.75 years, a reduction of 4.25 years. However, should you decide to overpay the full $250 per month, you will save just under $28,000 in interest charges over the same 25-year period, and the mortgage term will reduce from 25 years to just 16.5 years, a big reduction of 8.5 years over the life of the mortgage term. So clearly, overpaying can have a major positive impact on your financial wellbeing and mortgage economics, if you can afford to do so! However, it is worth pointing out that it doesn't always make sense to overpay on your mortgage. For example, if you have more expensive student loan and credit card debt outstanding, this should be prioritised as it is costing you more per month. This is the key point; your individual circumstances should dictate where you allocate your monthly savings.

FINAL THOUGHTS

Before running the analysis of a property purchase, it is important to evaluate the opportunity cost of committing your deposit too. For some people who are living in the family home and working locally, the rent trap concept doesn't necessarily apply, and so buying a property may not be top of mind. Equally, perhaps the experts are forecasting an imminent recession, in which case now may not be a great time to invest in property and you may find a better use elsewhere for your hard-earned capital!

In your research, try to avoid relying too much on people who have a clear bias or vested interest in talking the market higher, such as estate agents, property developers, and mortgage brokers. While it is great to pick their brain and hear the expert views, remember that some people rely on a vibrant property market in order to put bread on the table! They may try to sell you a narrative that 'this time is different', however keep in mind that markets move in cycles, and no sector is fully immune from the peaks and troughs, as we have seen in recent history! Do your own analysis and confide in people you trust and respect. This is a big commitment, and as all the people suffering with negative equity can attest, it is important you give yourself the best chance of success in terms of entry point. Agents will make money on at least one side of your property deal, so be sure that you fully understand their pricing structure and any hidden incentives for either party!

SAVING ACCOUNT

I want to touch on the main type of saving accounts in the market such as the regular saver and fixed rate saver among others. 1) The regular saver account is where you put a set amount aside every month, in order to avail of a higher interest rate offering compared with a standard savings account. Most banks will allow you to save up to $500 per month, and interest rates are typically around 1.5% for a full 12-month period. The downside is that you can't touch the money for the period, and in most cases any early withdrawal will forfeit the entire interest accrued! 2) The fixed rate saver is where you can lock in a predetermined interest rate for a set period such as 1, 2, or even 5 years. With rates at near record lows at the time of writing, there aren't too many people willing to lock in a savings account for 5 years! While last year it was possible to get a 12-month fixed rate at about 2%, right now you can't even get a 5-year fixed rate offering this amount, which underpins just how bleak the market is! Instead, one can expect to receive around 1% for a fixed rate savings account in the current environment, which will be higher than the regular saver given the sacrifice you are making to tie up your money for a prolonged period (the longer the term, the higher the interest rate received as a general rule)!

OTHERS - Other considerations should include evaluating any outstanding debt payments you have, as interest rates will likely be significantly higher on credit cards and overdrafts compared to potential saving rates earned. In my view, any surplus funds should first be used to pay off your most expensive interest rate debt as otherwise, you will likely lose money every month on your net interest rate differential. Another option is to use your savings to overpay on your mortgage either as an offset account (as we discussed earlier), or an outright overpayment. Overpaying on your mortgage balance can save you tens of thousands over the product duration as we have seen, however make sure there are no hidden penalties for doing so, as some banks are known to apply overpayment charges above a certain annual threshold, typically 10% of the outstanding balance.

To summarise, money required for emergency reasons including sudden job loss and illness belong in an easy access savings account. What you sacrifice in terms of competitive interest rates, you gain in ease of convenience and accessibility at short notice to provide liquidity for necessary 'rainy day' expenses over the next 6-12 months. Thereafter, the overall balance between saving and investing should be determined by setting a clear timeframe of your future goals and aspirations.

Over the medium term (time horizon of about 1-5 years forward), it often makes sense to move excess savings into an investment account where you can put your money to work, in order to achieve a return in excess of your savings rate. At the same time, you can also ensure relative ease of access (and liquidity) for expenses such as a family wedding, education, car purchase, or deposit for a house among other life events. Of course, you can predetermine your risk appetite to ensure your portfolio volatility is commensurate with your desired lifestyle, because let's face it there is always going to be bubbles, corrections, and recessions from time to time. The key is to stick with a diversified, high quality portfolio over the long term. While in the short term, your exposure to investment risk means you can lose money, you should expect to generate a positive return well in excess of the bank savings rate over the medium to long term. In addition, you should also consider inflation risk, as inflation typically runs between 2-3% annually, meaning any return below this 2-3% hurdle will have you losing money and purchasing power. Investing doesn't have to be intimidating, and when done sensibly (as part of a diversified portfolio, without margin or borrowing, and a long-term approach), investing can prove rewarding and stimulating!

Finally, funds required over the long term (time horizon of 10+ years), should ideally be invested directly into a long-term retirement fund strategy (or equivalent) concentrated in a basket of globally diversified equities, bonds, and alternative assets, such as commodities and property as we discussed earlier. As a general rule, the younger you are, the higher the allocation to equities and risk assets compared with bonds and other fixed income producing assets, as you are further away from retirement and loss of income (at least in theory)!

THE NEW NORMAL

While it's easy to talk about saving for the future, the reality is that most people are struggling to get by day to day, given the trend of rising inequality, unemployment, and wage stagnation. For example, in the UK as many as 1 in 3 people have less than £1,500 in the bank, while close to 15% of the population are living hand to mouth without any savings, according to recent statistics. In addition, over 50% of adults don't contribute to a regular monthly savings plan, with the majority citing a lack of income as the primary reason. In addition, close to 70% of the population do not make an annual financial plan to help determine their financial objectives. Clearly, these broad trends are not unique to the UK and affect us all.

According to one survey conducted by the Royal Society of Arts, economic uncertainty has become a 'new normal' in the UK, with close to 70% of the population fitting into the 'chronically broke' category. The survey was conducted with 2,000 workers across a broad spectrum of the economy, and showed a third of workers had less than

£500 savings, 40% reported their finances as being permanently close to collapse, while 30% of participants stated they were unable to get by each month. For me, the survey confirmed the growing trend of inequality, and the vast divergence between healthy economic indicators reported in the press compared to the harsh realities on the ground. The majority of our society is only one emergency health incident or unpaid child-care bill away from collapse, leaving little wonder why as many as 70% of workers report regular stress and a lack of autonomy.

At the same time, the millennial generation in particular 'face a series of difficulties in building wealth…due to the combined impact of rising house prices, insecure employment and higher debt, including student debt', according to a recent study by the FCA. To make matters worse, the report emphasised millennials were unlikely to have repaid their mortgages by the time they reached their 60s, unlike the baby-boomers who typically enjoy a debt-free retirement. As a by-product, it is the younger generation who suffer most from an economic crisis such as Covid-19, as their job security is far more vulnerable, often stuck on variable contracts with little to no benefits. In fact, the Office for National Statistics (ONS) found that 25 million people in the UK (close to half the population) experienced high anxiety as the country went into Covid-19 lockdown. Close to 10 million people suffered a hit to income almost immediately, with most either renters or the self-employed, or both. In addition, the ONS found that life satisfaction scores were at the lowest level since surveys began in 2011. Not surprisingly, finances and employment were among people's biggest concerns, while the young were disproportionately affected once again!

MIND THE GAP

Another prevalent savings issue is the gender gap. In the UK, 1 in 4 adult males have over £20,000 in savings, compared to less than 1 in 5 females. While it is well publicised that men traditionally carry a wage premium in the work force, there are clear indications this is finally diminishing. Interestingly, the UK also suffers from a big location gap when it comes to savings. In London for example, almost 70% of workers add to their savings on a monthly basis, with a large majority using advanced technological platforms to achieve their financial goals. By contrast, large parts of northern England report no savings at all. According to some reports, low income families have less than £100 in savings, compared to the higher income households with over £50,000 in the bank (excluding the value of both groups' respective home). Close to 90% of high-income families are homeowners, while only 40% of low-income families can say the same, and these recent trends are only getting more amplified over time. Take the current post Covid-19 environment, where low income professionals are disproportionately affected by job loss and economic recession, while the higher income categories are more likely to benefit from recovering stock markets and house price indicators.

Finally, for the younger demographic in the UK, over 50% of people age 22-29 have no savings at all to their name (according to ONS figures). The top 10% cohort of savers have over £15,000 savings in the bank, while the bottom

10% have less than £100 set aside, with the average set at £2,000. Related to this savings issue is thorny topic of home ownership, which has fallen sharply since the 2007/08 financial crisis. Only 25% of this age group are homeowners, 35% still live with their parents, while the remainder are stuck in rented accommodation. The reality is that homeownership is unattainable for the vast majority when you consider that close to 70% earn less than £30,000 per year, and the average house price in the UK is slightly over £250,000, making it almost impossible to qualify for a mortgage with an average house price to income ratio of 8.33x (typical mortgage multiple is 4.5x). Unfortunately, this underpins much of what is wrong in our ever-fragmented society!

QUOTES ON MONEY

'He that is of the opinion that money will do everything may well be suspected of doing everything for money' – Benjamin Franklin

'Don't save what is left after spending; instead spend what is left after saving' – Warren Buffett

'I don't look to jump over seven-foot bars; I look around for one-foot bars that I can step over' – Warren Buffett

'Money is like manure; it's not worth a thing unless it's spread around encouraging young things to grow' – Thornton Wilder

'Don't look for the needle in the haystack. Just buy the haystack!' – John Bogle

***

Top 10 Book Recommendations

Leonardo Da Vinci by Walter Isaacson

Benjamin Franklin by Walter Isaacson

The Fountainhead by Ayn Rand

Einstein by Walter Isaacson

FDR by Jean Edward Smith

Outliers by Malcolm Gladwell

Team of Rivals by Doris Kearns Goodwin

Animal Farm by George Orwell

The Catcher in the Rye by JD Salinger

Open by Andre Agassi

Special thanks to all who contributed – you know who you are!

Printed in Great Britain
by Amazon